DECORATING
TABLE LINENS

Detail of place mat, page 93.

DECORATING

TABLE LINENS

60 TABLECLOTHS, PLACE MATS, AND NAPKINS
TO APPLIQUÉ, PAINT, CROSS-STITCH, EMBROIDER, AND SEW

CHRIS RANKIN

A Sterling/Lark Book
Sterling Publishing Co., Inc.   New York

Editor: Carol Taylor
Design: Sandra Montgomery, Marcia Winters
Translations: Networks, Inc.
Editorial assistance: Nola Theiss
Production: Sandra Montgomery, Elaine Thompson
Illustrations: Charlie Covington

Library of Congress Cataloging-in-Publication Data
Rankin, Chris.
   Decorating table linens : 60 tablecloths, place mats, and napkins
to applique, paint, cross stitch, embroider, and sew / Chris Rankin.
     p.   cm.
  "A Sterling/Lark book."
  Includes index.
  ISBN 0-8069-8598-4
   1. Needlework.   2. Household linens.   3. Textile painting.
I. Title
TT751.R36   1992
746.9'6--dc20   91-38787
                                         CIP

ISBN 0-8069-8598-4

10   9   8   7   6   5   4   3   2   1

A Sterling/Lark Book

Produced by Altamont Press, Inc.
50 College St., Asheville, NC 28801

Published in 1992 by Sterling Publishing Co., Inc.
387 Park Ave. S., New York, NY 10016

© 1992, Altamont Press

Distributed in Canada by Sterling Publishing,
c/o Canadian Manda Group, P.O. Box 920, Station U, Toronto,
   Ontario M8Z 5P9
Distributed in the United Kingdom by Cassell PLC, Villiers House,
   41/47 Strand, London WC2N 5JE, England
Distributed in Australia by Capricorn Link Ltd., P.O. Box 665,
   Lane Cove, NSW 2066

Printed in Hong Kong

TABLE OF CONTENTS

INTRODUCTION

The most elemental fact of human existence is that we must eat to stay alive. This mundane certainty requires us to work, cook, shop, scour, garden—to invest enormous energy in obtaining the food we must have.

It does not require us to stencil a tablecloth.

But we do. And when we do, we are in excellent company. We join the pioneer woman making quilts by candlelight, inventing complex and lovely patterns as she pieces together the scraps that will keep her family warm. We join the furniture maker building grace and charm into chairs and tables for no other reason than he likes them that way. We join the basket weaver wading along a muddy creek bank, searching for the wild plants that will dye the reed rich, warm colors.

In short, we join the ancient tradition of folk art, of ordinary people decorating everyday objects. Perhaps our most endearing human trait is this impulse to save just a bit of energy and just a few hours to make the useful beautiful.

The projects in this book use painting and stencilling, sewing and applique, cross stitch and embroidery. There's not a new technique among them. Our great grandmothers (and some of our grandfathers) were usually competent and often expert.

But there are some new refinements. No stenciller has to face carbon and cardboard any more. Modern fabric paints have opened up new vistas of creativity. Even stitchery gets easier with the years.

This book presumes you know how to thread a needle, machine-stitch a straight seam, and hand-sew a hem—no more. It includes general directions and specific instructions for tablecloths, place mats, napkins, table runners, egg warmers, and tea cozies. (Yes, tea cozies. Do *you* like tepid tea?) Projects range from quick and easy to those that demand more time.

Table linens are a joy to decorate. They lend themselves to a variety of techniques, and fabrics are available in so many colors and textures that your options are practically unlimited. And when you've finished your table linens, you can invite people over to sit and look at them—through as many courses as you like.

Instructions for this project are found on page 27.

TABLE LINENS: THE BASICS

MAKING YOUR OWN

All of the techniques and projects in this book can be worked on purchased table linen. For an even wider choice of color and fabric, you can make your own, with very little time or trouble.

FABRICS

Keep in mind that table linens can receive some hard wear. They get abraded with heavy dinnerware, stabbed with sharp forks, and assaulted with garlic butter. Choose fabrics that not only look good but that wash well—or least dry clean easily. If the fabric resists stains and wrinkles, so much the better. Obviously, a cloth for a decorative corner table can be more delicate than the covering in a functional breakfast nook. Also consider how you intend to decorate the cloth, and make sure the fabric will cooperate.

There's a reason it's known as "table linen." Linen is the classic fabric, and it's beautiful for many applications, if somewhat difficult to care for. Cotton and cotton/synthetic blends work well and are available in a wide array of prints and solid colors. For truly formal settings, consider the traditional damask or lace.

TABLECLOTHS

When you come right down to it, a tablecloth is a piece of fabric with a hem. There is no simpler sewing project. If you can hold your edge around a pair of scissors and look a needle in the eye, you have the skills and the tools you need.

MEASURING

You'll need enough fabric to account for three things: the tabletop, the drop, and the hem.

1. Measure the length and width of a rectangular tabletop, or the diameter of one that's round or square.

2. Decide how far you want the cloth to drop from the edge of the table. An obvious method is to pull up a chair you normally use at this table and measure from the tabletop to your lap. In general, a shorter drop will look skimpy and a longer one will increase the odds that you'll clear the table by sitting on the tablecloth. For a more generous drop, measure to the chair seat.

For a floor-length cloth, measure the distance from the tabletop to 1/2" above the floor.

3. A tablecloth doesn't require a wide hem. Usually, 1/2" to 1", with a 1/4" inner hem, is ample. If you prefer a deeper hem, by all means make one. The cloth will hang more solidly and will acquire more visual weight.

CALCULATING AMOUNTS

To determine the amount of fabric you need, add *twice* the drop length to both the length and width measurements (or to the diameter of a round table) and *twice* the total hem (outer and inner).

If the fabric is wide enough to accommodate the total width requirements for the tablecloth, just buy a piece long enough to take care of the total length requirements. If the fabric isn't as wide as the tablecloth—for example, if you're buying 45" wide fabric and making a 60" wide tablecloth—allow twice the total length requirements. (See "Piecing.")

PIECING

A tablecloth cut from one piece of fabric is the easiest to make and the most convenient to use—there are no seams to make a wine glass tipsy. It's also far more attractive to decorate. If the tablecloth is wider than the fabric, you've got two choices. One is to make a center panel with equal side panels. The other is to put a seam down the center of the table.

A center panel is usually better, especially if the tablecloth will be painted, appliquéd, or embroidered. The point is to have an unseamed canvas to work on, and most people place their decorative motifs on the tabletop.

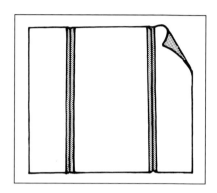

On the other hand, if you intend to leave the top of the cloth bare and place your motifs around the sides, you might consider running the seam down the center of the cloth. (Traditionalists argue that a tablecloth should *never* have a center seam, but those are the same people who won't let you serve red wine with chicken even if you really want to.)

To make a cloth with a center seam, just sew the two lengths of fabric together. Place them right sides together, and machine-stitch down one long side, leaving a 1/2" seam allowance.

For a center panel, cut one length of fabric in half lengthwise, and sew one half to each side of the central panel. Again, place the pieces right sides together and stitch, leaving a 1/2" seam allowance.

CUTTING A ROUND TABLECLOTH

It is remarkably reassuring to try this with an ordinary piece of paper before taking scissors to fabric.

1. Cut a square of fabric with sides the same length as the diameter of the circle you need. For example, if you need a circle 60" across, cut a square with 60" sides. Fold the square in quarters,

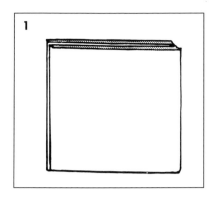

taking note of which corner is the center of the fabric. That's corner A.

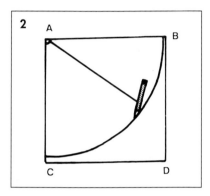

2. Cut a piece of paper the same size as the folded square. Find a piece of string and tie one end to a pencil and the other end to a pin. The distance between the pin and the pencil should equal the radius of the tablecloth (half the diameter). Stick the pin in corner A of the paper and swing the pencil around in an arc from corner B to corner D, creating a quarter circle. Pin the pattern on the fabric.

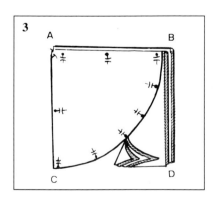

3. Cut along the rounded edge of the pattern, through all four layers of fabric.

4. Remove the pattern, and unfold your circle.

PLACE MATS

A great place mat will accommodate one place setting and two elbows.

Of course, the mats can be any size. If you have one that you're particularly fond of, measure it. If you don't, set out your dishes, lean on the table as if lost in after-dinner conversation, and measure how much space you've used.

The simplest place mat is a rectangular or oval piece of cloth with a hem. A 1/2" hem with a 1/4" inner hem is ample, sewn by hand or machine. A bias-binding hem looks particularly good on place mats (see "Using Bias Binding").

If the fabric is flimsy, you may want to line the place mat with the same fabric or with a complementary color. Cut two pieces of fabric 1" longer and wider than the finished mat, lay them right sides together, and machine stitch around the edge, with a 1/2" seam allowance. Leave a 3" opening on one side, and turn the mat right side out through the opening. Then hand-sew the opening closed. If you like, you can finish the mat with a row of topstitching an inch from the edge (just machine-stitch around the mat on the right side).

NAPKINS

Like place mats, napkins can be any size, but they're usually between 12 and 16 inches square. You might take into consideration the amount of fabric you've got and the eating habits of your friends. Cut the fabric the size you want, leaving a 1/2" hem allowance, then make a 1/4" hem with a 1/4" inner hem.

MITERED CORNERS

The only trick to hemming a square or rectangular piece of fabric is dealing with the corners. To make corners smooth, flat, and neat, just miter them—a simple technique that's immensely satisfying.

The easiest way to visualize how mitering works is to fold up a piece of paper, pretending all the while that it's a lavishly decorated tablecloth.

Whatever the width of your hem, add about 1/4" for an inner hem.

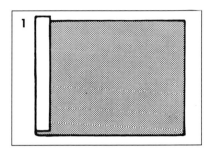

1. Fold the 1/4" inner hem to the wrong side, and press it.

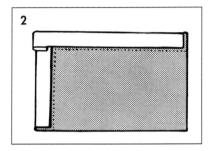

2. Fold over the outer hem of the tablecloth, and press it to form a crease. Open the outer hem, so you're left with a folded inner hem and an ironed crease where the hemline will be.

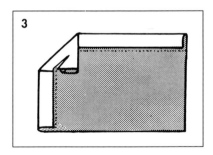

3. Fold over a corner so that its fold line passes through the point where two pressed creases intersect, and iron in place. Leaving a 1/4" seam allowance, cut off the corner.

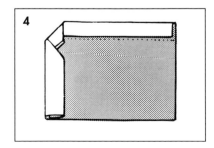

4. On one edge, turn over the outer hem along the pressed crease. Pin in place.

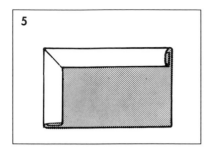

5. Fold the other hem along the pressed hemline. The two edges will meet to form a diagonal seam at the corner. Pin the corner in place, and sew up the diagonal seam with a slipstitch.

USING BIAS BINDING

Finishing a tablecloth or place mat with commercial bias binding is a quick alternative to the ordinary hem. Bias binding looks especially good on a casual cloth or a bright-colored one.

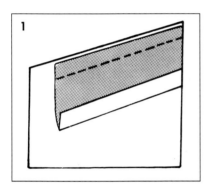

Open one folded edge of the double-folded binding, and pin it around the tablecloth, with right sides together and raw edges level. Machine stitch in place along the crease in the binding.

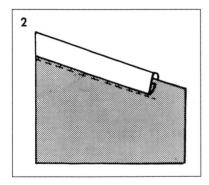

Fold the binding over the cloth to the wrong side, and pin in place. Either hemstitch the binding to the cloth by hand, as you would an ordinary hem, or topstitch by machine on the right side.

OPENWORK HEMS

Several of the tablecloths in later chapters have an openwork border above the hem. As attractive as these borders are, they're strictly optional. If you substitute an ordinary hem, the project will be complete.

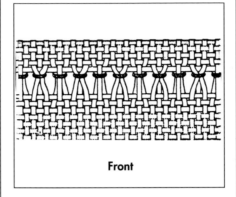

Front

If you want an openwork border, here's how to do it. First, make sure you're working on fabric with threads you can count. If you are, find a horizontal thread the desired distance from the top of the hem. Thread a needle with matching sewing thread, and use the needle to wrap the sewing thread around 2 to 4 vertical threads of the

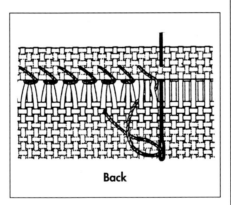

Back

fabric. Pull tightly. Continue across, carefully following the horizontal thread. You may have to adjust the number of threads to make the corner hole fall exactly at the corner. When sewing the hem, you may want to wrap the hemming stitches around the openwork stitches as well.

PAINT

For fabric lovers, the recent explosion of fabric paints has been a marvelous development. Widely available in a rainbow of colors, fast and easy to use, fabric paints have opened up whole new craft possibilities.

FREE-HAND PAINTING

Painting on fabric is like painting on anything else. You dip a paint brush in the paint and brush it on the fabric. Wide brushes produce broad strokes, narrow-tipped brushes give you finer lines. Nothing could be simpler. There are just a few tricks.

1. Wash and iron the fabric first, to remove any sizing and provide a wrinkle-free canvas.

2. Read the instructions on the paint bottle. Some manufacturers recommend diluting their paints with thinner or even water.

3. Most fabric paints must be heat-set with an iron after they're dry or they'll wash out during laundering. Again, check the label.

4. Paint tends to bleed through fabric. It's a good idea to put several layers of newspaper or rags underneath the fabric before you start to work.

5. If you want to use a pre-drawn design, so that you can color within the lines, draw or trace the pattern onto a piece of paper, using a black felt-tip pen. Place the drawing under the fabric and leave it there while you paint. Many fabrics are sheer enough so that the design will show through, at least dimly.

Another choice is to transfer the outline onto the fabric itself. Trace the motif onto tracing paper, then turn the paper to the back side and go over the lines with a transfer pencil (available with sewing, quilting, and craft supplies). Lay the design on the fabric with the transfer side down, and press with a warm iron.

5. Many designs look better if the broad areas of color are accented with darker, finer lines—for example, dark green veins to set off light green leaves. These accents can be embroidered, painted with a narrow brush and a darker color of paint, or sketched in with a fabric marker pen.

Just because some of the projects in Chapter 2 have been accented with embroidery doesn't mean you have to pick up a needle. Painted accents will work just as well.

STENCILLING

Stencilled designs have enormous charm. Partly it's their old-time, folk art look, partly it's our own perceptual pleasure: when we look at them, we create a visual whole out of disconnected parts.

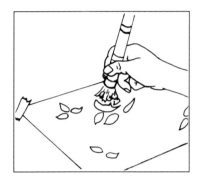

EQUIPMENT

Elaborate equipment is not required. First, you'll need something to make the stencil out of—something that's easy to cut, impervious to paint, and transparent.

Oiled stencilling paper looks and feels like ordinary waxed paper that's into body building. Its waxy texture prevents paint from bleeding through anywhere except the cut-out areas, it cuts cleanly even in fine detail, and it's transparent enough that bold black lines show through clearly. It's inexpensive and available in craft stores.

Clear acetate is a flexible plastic that comes in letter-sized sheets. It cuts easily (although not as docilely as paper) and is completely transparent; everything shows through. Acetate is sold in craft shops and office supply stores.

To cut the stencil, you'll need a pencil-sized *craft knife* with a sharp blade. It cuts straight and curved lines, large and small areas. Hold it as you would a pencil.

Stubby *stencilling brushes* have blunt-cut ends, for applying small amounts of paint as smoothly as possible. They come in a variety of widths.

You'll also need a *felt-tip pen* that will mark cleanly on waxy paper or acetate (if in doubt, ask the salesperson for advice), *masking tape, fabric paint,* and a small saucer or *dish* for each color of paint.

PROCEDURES

First, check to see that the design you want to stencil is the size you want it. Use a photocopy machine with a sizing capacity to enlarge the design if necessary.

Lay the stencilling paper or acetate on the design, and trace over the lines with the felt-tip pen. Leave a margin of 2" or so, to reduce the chances of accidentally getting paint on the fabric. With the craft knife, cut out the areas to be painted. Position the stencil on the fabric, and tape its corners with masking tape.

Stencilling requires very little paint. A few tablespoons will stencil a border around the walls of a large room; a tablecloth takes only a dribble. You want to work with a brush that's almost dry, to prevent smudges and to produce the characteristic stencilled look.

Dribble some fabric paint into a saucer, and use your stencilling brush to swirl it around until you've got a thin layer. Dab the wet brush onto a paper towel until it's almost dry. Then, holding the brush upright, dab the paint into the cutout areas. Avoid the brush strokes you would use in other kinds of painting. Instead, dab the paint on. Each time you add more paint to your brush, clean it off on a paper towel before starting work.

When you lift the stencil to check the design or to move it to another area, be careful not to smudge the paint. The edges of the design should be as sharp as you can make them. And wipe any excess paint off the stencil before you lay it back down on the tablecloth.

MULTIPLE COLORS

If your design has more than one color, you'll need to make a separate stencil for each one. One stencil would have all the red areas, another would

have all the green, and so on. Each color is then painted one at a time.

Multiple stencils must be positioned accurately as you paint, so that the design hangs together. Registration marks will help. When you trace the stencil for the first color, mark a dot on either side of the overall design. Before you trace the second color, lay the acetate over the first stencil and copy those two dots. When you cut the stencils, cut out the dots as well. Then, when you position the first stencil on the cloth, make light pencil marks through the registration holes. Use those marks to position the second stencil. Follow the same procedure for subsequent colors.

APPLIQUE

Although appliques can be stitched on by hand, a sewing machine supplies a surer bond and cuts the time required at least by half.

Template. First, make a template. If the pattern isn't full size, enlarge it on a photocopy machine. Cut out the enlarged image, and you have a template. If the motif shown in the book is the size you want, trace it onto tracing paper. Then cut out the motif—again, your template. (An alternative is to trace the pattern onto tracing paper, then pin the uncut paper to the fabric, positioning the motif where you want it.)

Note that if an appliquéd design has more than one part, you'll have to make a template for each separate piece.

Cutting. If you've already cut out the template, pin it to the right side of the applique fabric, and trace around it. Remove the pattern, leaving the outlined shape, and cut out the applique. If you've pinned the uncut tracing paper to the fabric, cut out the motif through paper and fabric simultaneously.

Interfacing. Most appliques look better if you add interfacing. While this is especially true of lightweight material, any applique looks more three-dimensional with a layer of interfacing underneath. Lay the applique fabric on a piece of interfacing, the template on top, and cut out both layers at once.

The easiest to use is iron-on (fusible) interfacing. Lay the cut applique on the cut interfacing, and press with a hot iron to seal the two together. (Follow the manufacturer's instructions.)

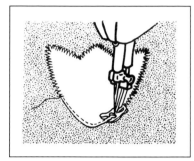

Sewing. Place the fabric applique on right side of background fabric, and pin the middle of the applique to hold it in place. With a narrow, short zigzag stitch, sew around the edges of the applique.

STITCHERY

NEEDLES

Most widely used are *crewel* needles—sharp, medium-length needles with large eyes. Their sizes range from 1 to 10 (the larger the number, the smaller the needle). Sharp *chenilles* (sizes 13 to 26) are thicker and longer and have larger eyes. They are designed for heavier yarns. *Tapestry* needles (sizes 13 to 26) are blunt, which makes them appropriate for thread-counting embroidery, such as cross stitch.

THREAD

Embroidery floss is a loosely twisted, six-stranded cotton that can be used as one thread or divided for finer work. Floss usually comes in skeins of 26 to 27 feet.

Pearl cotton is a twisted, two-ply thread that cannot be divided. It is more lustrous than floss and comes in skeins or balls.

HOOPS

Essential for unpuckered results, an embroidery hoop holds the fabric taut while you work. A hoop consists of two wooden or plastic rings, one fit-

ting inside the other. The outer ring has an opening that can be tightened or loosened by means of a screw.

To mount the fabric in a hoop, first place the fabric, design side up, over the inner ring, then press the outer ring down around the inner one. Adjust the fabric so that it's smooth and taut, then tighten the screw to make the unit secure.

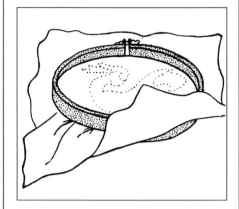

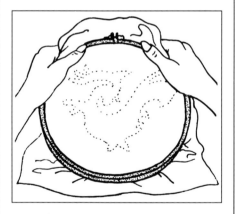

FABRICS

Most fabrics for embroidery fall into two categories. **Common-weave fabrics** are tightly woven cloths with smooth surfaces—for example, linen, wool, cotton, and synthetics. All are appropriate for free-form embroidery.

Even-weave fabrics have the same number of warp and weft threads in each square inch. This means that the woven threads form a grid. A *single even-weave* has single intersecting threads. Depending on the thickness of the threads, the fabric can vary from fine to coarse. *Hardanger cloth,* recommended for several projects in later chapters, is an even-weave fabric with pairs of threads that intersect, usually

between 22 and 28 pairs per inch. *Aida cloth* has intersecting groups of threads, usually 11 to the inch.

The grid of even-weave fabric is critical to techniques such as cross stitch. Cross stitch patterns come in two forms. First, there are the hot-iron transfers common to all types of embroidery (see below). If you're working from a hot-iron transfer, you can work cross stitch on any fabric suitable for embroidery.

The second type of cross stitch pattern is the chart, itself a kind of grid on which each square represents one intersection of threads or thread groups. Squares of the pattern are filled in with symbols that stand for colors—for example, a dash for yellow and a V for orange. Since there's nothing printed on the cloth itself, a fabric with a uniform grid is essential. Since the cross stitch projects in this book are presented in chart form, the directions recommend even-weave fabrics such as hardanger or Aida cloth.

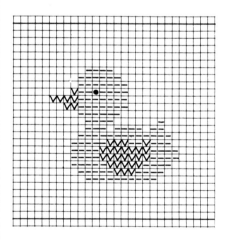

If hardanger and Aida cloth are difficult to find in your area, or if you simply don't want to use them, use whatever fabric you want and create a temporary grid with needlepoint canvas. Select an appropriate size of either plain mono or penelope canvas (avoid interlocking meshes) and baste it to the embroidery fabric. Work the design according to the chart, then remove the basting and trim the excess canvas as close to the embroidery as possible, being careful not to cut the stitches. Then dismantle your grid. Starting from one corner, carefully draw out all parallel threads of canvas in one direction. Then, working from another corner, draw out the remaining threads. You'll be left with a perfectly gridded pattern.

TRANSFERRING DESIGNS

The designs in this book can be transferred to the fabric in several ways. One of the easiest methods is to use a transfer pencil, available in craft, quilting, and embroidery supply stores.

Trace the design onto heavy tracing paper (the oiled stencilling paper you're going to buy for Chapter 2 will be perfect). Turn the paper over and, on the back, trace over the lines with the transfer pencil. Place the paper, traced side down, on the fabric, turn iron to low setting, and press down on the pattern for a few seconds. Lift the iron, then move to the next area of the design. Don't slide the iron back and forth, or the lines may smear.

A second option is dressmaker's carbon, which comes in packets of several likeable colors. (Avoid typewriter carbon paper, which tends to smear.) Place the pattern right side up on the fabric, and pin it at the corners. Slip the carbon paper, carbon side down, between the pattern and the fabric. Draw over the lines of the pattern, using a blunt-tipped object such as a knitting needle.

STARTING AND STOPPING

Don't use regular sewing knots. Instead, begin the first thread by leaving a "tail" on the wrong side. As you embroider, catch the tail in the stitching for about two inches. To start the next new thread, slide the thread through a row of stitches on the wrong side, near the spot to be embroidered.

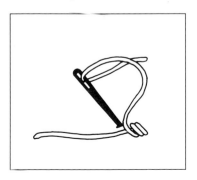

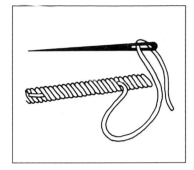

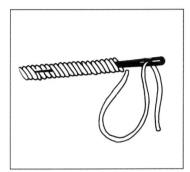

To end a thread, pull it through to the wrong side and slip the needle through a row of stitches for about two inches, then cut off the thread.

EMBROIDERY STITCHES

BACK STITCH

A common outline stitch. Bring needle to right side along design line, take a small stitch backward, and bring needle to right side again in front of the first stitch, a stitch length away. Continue along the design line, always finishing stitch by inserting needle at point where last stitch began.

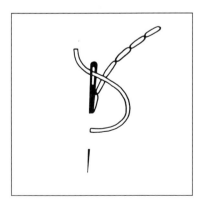

BLANKET STITCH

A finishing stitch for edges, and an outlining stitch when worked small. Bring needle to right side at point A

and insert above and to the right at point B. Bring needle to right side again at C, with thread under tip of needle, and pull thread through. Continue in this manner, with last point of stitch always acting as first point of next stitch. To finish blanket stitch, insert needle next to loop (see below).

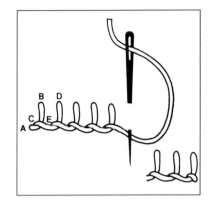

BUTTONHOLE STITCH

Blanket stitches worked close together to form a sturdy edge. Most frequently used for cutwork embroidery and buttonholes.

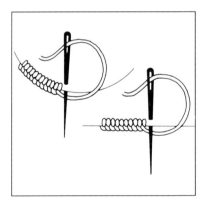

CHAIN STITCH

Used for both outlining and filling. Draw (or imagine) a line to be covered. Bring thread to right side along

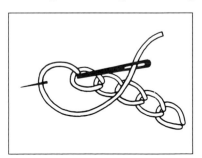

line, and hold down with left thumb. Insert needle where it last exited and bring point out a short distance away along line, with thread under tip of needle. Pull thread through. Continue, always keeping the working thread beneath tip of needle.

DAISY STITCH

A stitch most often used for flowers. Bring needle to the front at 1, then go back through the same hole and exit again at 2. Carry yarn under tip of needle and pull through. Insert needle at 3 over loop, then bring needle out to start next chain stitch.

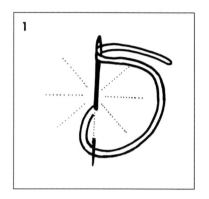

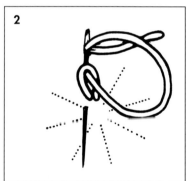

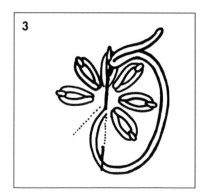

CROSS STITCHES

As the name suggests, all cross stitches consist of two crossing arms.

BASIC CROSS STITCH

Usually worked in rows. Work from right to left, laying down half the crosses, then back from left to right (see first two drawings). If you prefer, you can work one cross at a time.

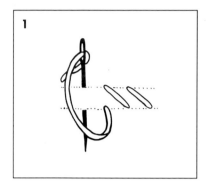

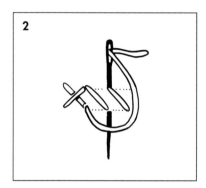

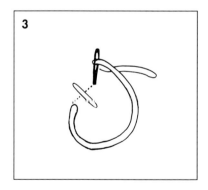

STAR STITCH
(DOUBLE CROSS STITCH)

Can fill an area or serve as a border. Bring needle out to right side and take a diagonal stitch. Bring needle out

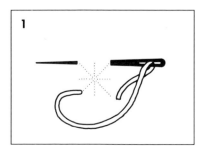

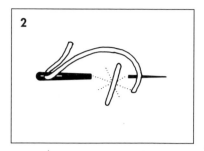

directly below end of stitch and take another diagonal stitch across center of first diagonal. Bring needle out at midpoint of two lower points of star,

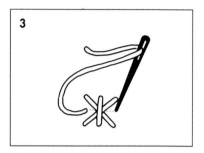

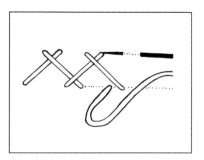

and cross center. Complete star by bringing needle out at side midpoint, then crossing center. The result should be a star contained in a perfect square.

HERRINGBONE STITCH

Popular for borders. Working from left to right, bring the needle to the front, take a slanting stitch up and to the right, then bring the needle out again a short distance back to the left. Finish the stitch by exiting to the lower right.

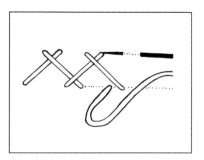

DOUBLE HERRINGBONE

To make a double herringbone, interlace a second row of herringbone with the first row. The two rows are often worked in contrasting thread. Bring the needle to the right side at A, right

1

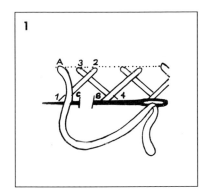

above 1, and insert it at B, right below 2, crossing over arm 1-2 in original

2

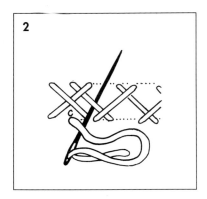

3

row. Bring needle to the front at C, and pass needle under arm 3-4 of the original row. Insert needle at D and exit at E.

FRENCH KNOT

A raised stitch that adds texture, often used for the centers of flowers. Bring needle to right side. Hold thread taut with left hand and wrap thread around point of needle twice. Pull thread tight around needle, and insert needle where it came out, holding thread taut

to form a clean knot. You can make larger knots by adding more twists of thread around needle.

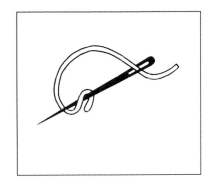

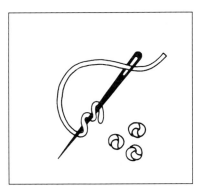

Detail of tablecloth, page 91.

BASIC RUNNING STITCH

Bring needle to right side and work from right to left, picking up the same number of threads for each stitch. If the fabric isn't too heavy, you can pick up several stitches on the needle before the thread is pulled through.

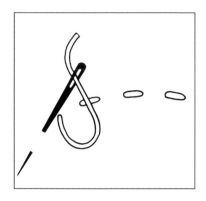

DOUBLE RUNNING STITCH (HOLBEIN)

Like the basic running stitch, the Holbein is used for outlining. It consists of two passes of running stitch, one on top of the other. First work evenly spaced running stitches, then turn the fabric over and work a second time, so that the stitches fill in the gaps left by the first pass.

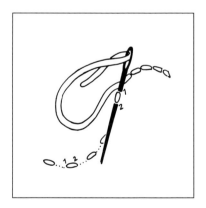

SATIN STITCH

The most popular stitch for filling solid areas. The idea is to work flat, even stitches that completely cover the fabric.

Bring needle to right side at lower side of band to be covered. Insert needle directly above its previous exit point, and pull thread through.

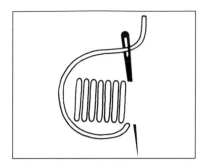

PADDED SATIN STITCH

Adds dimension to the design. First work the outline of design in split or chain stitch. Next, carefully cover design with a horizontal satin stitch, working just to outside edge of outline stitch. Then work satin stitch over design again, in any direction other than the horizontal already used.

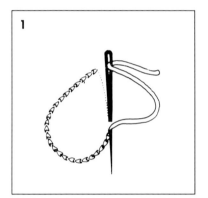

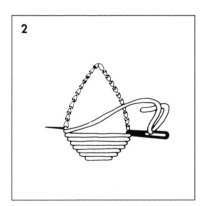

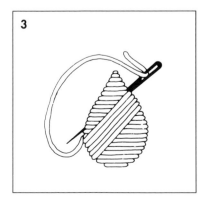

SPLIT STITCH

Used for either outlining or filling, for a fine, flat surface. Bring needle to right side along design line, insert needle a short distance away, and bring it out again, piercing previous stitch.

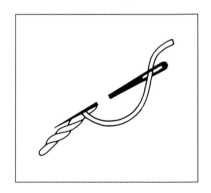

STEM STITCH

A favorite outline stitch often used to work stems of flowers and leaves. Working along a line, bring needle out to right side. Insert needle along line

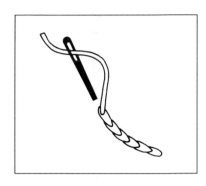

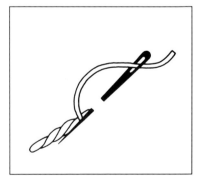

to right, then bring it back out half a stitch length back. For a wider stitch, angle needle slightly.

PAINT

Summer roses bloom everywhere on this table setting. Those on the table-cloth are stencilled in colorful fabric paint. In the areas between the rose motifs, spatter painting—accomplished with a toothbrush and a piece of screen-ing—provides interesting highlights and ties the motifs together. For a matching chair, use the same stencil but substitute a paint appropriate for wood.

INSTRUCTIONS FOR THIS PROJECT
ARE FOUND ON PAGE 28.

PAINT

Not all painted fabrics are stencilled. This handsome tablecloth, with its restrained color scheme and understated design, was painted free-hand. The designer mixed black and transparent white paint in various proportions, used a 3" wide brush, and changed the direction of the brush strokes with every square

INSTRUCTIONS FOR THIS PROJECT ARE FOUND ON PAGE 28.

PAINT

An ordinary white cotton tablecloth can become as special as a midday meal of fresh bread and red wine. The stencilled grapes are shaded with purple and brown, to suggest varying degrees of ripeness, and the leaves are stencilled in both positive and negative images. Some of the cut-out areas of the stencil are filled completely and some left only partially painted, which adds interesting variety to the motif

INSTRUCTIONS FOR THIS PROJECT ARE FOUND ON PAGES 28 AND 35.

PAINT

S tencilled lemons and oranges plus bright blue rickrack make a cloth that's perfect for a cheerful breakfast or a leisurely lunch. The tablecloth shown has been accented with embroidery on the stems and shaded areas of the fruit, but painted accents would be just as lively.

INSTRUCTIONS FOR THIS PROJECT ARE FOUND ON PAGE 30.

PAINT

I f you have car-crazy kids (or grown-ups) in your house, this tablecloth will drive them to the dinner table and keep them there. In fact, they can help paint it.

Just buy or make a plain white cotton table-cloth, and stencil it in bright primary colors, using a separate stencil for each color. A bias-binding hem in a matching hue is a perfect finishing touch.

INSTRUCTIONS FOR THIS PRO-JECT ARE FOUND ON PAGE 31.

PAINT

Bright-colored eggs are a wonderful Easter tradition. Kids love to dye them, hide them, and then find them. For your egg-dyeing party, stencil a tablecloth, a tea cozy, even some egg warmers in an Easter egg motif.

INSTRUCTIONS FOR THIS PROJECT ARE FOUND ON PAGE 32.

PAINT

*C*ombining *two colors of paint can add depth and interest, as on both the projects shown on these pages. For a blended effect, paint the flowers on the tablecloth lightly in red, and allow them to dry. Then brush white paint over the red, to create a washed salmon color. For the tulips on the napkins, mix red and white to get pink, but don't mix completely.*

Both projects are shown highlighted with embroidery. A row of stem stitch borders the tablecloth; the tulip napkins have a chain stitch border and embroidered accents on the flowers. But the needlework is optional. If you'd rather stay with paint, just add the accent lines with a narrow-tipped brush and a darker shade of fabric paint. The borders can be omitted or painted very effectively (see the directions).

INSTRUCTIONS FOR THESE PROJECTS ARE FOUND ON PAGES 33 AND 34.

PAINT

S ome of the best "table linen" is actually "table paper." If you plan a holiday party for children or particularly jolly adults, try a table setting that mimics cross stitch.

Outline a chubby snow person on graph paper. Then paint the face, hat, scarf, and perhaps the buttons in what pass for the appropriate places. Cut out the cast of characters, and glue them to bright paper place mats and napkins.

INSTRUCTIONS FOR THIS PROJECT ARE FOUND ON PAGE 35.

Tablecloth
With Chickens

PAGE 6

FINISHED MEASUREMENTS
60" x 60"

MATERIALS
2-1/2 yds unbleached cotton fabric 60" wide, 1-3/4 yds dark pink checked fabric 45" wide, stencilling paper or clear acetate, felt-tip pen, craft knife, masking tape, fabric paint in rose, blue, white, and black, small saucers or bowls for mixing paint, stencilling brush

INSTRUCTIONS

From the unbleached fabric, cut a 40" x 40" square and 4 strips 9-1/2" x 60". From the checked fabric, cut 4 strips 9-1/2" x 60".

With felt-tip pen, trace the hen, the heart, and the dot onto stencilling paper or acetate. Cut out the motifs with the craft knife.

In saucers, mix the rose and blue paints, and the black and white paints, to get desired colors. Test the colors on the edge of the saucer and then on a piece of scratch paper, until you get colors you like. Dip brush in mixed paint, and wipe off excess paint on paper towel. Brush should be almost dry.

Position stencil on unbleached cotton square and tape the stencil's corners. Begin 2-1/2" from lower edge. Paint a heart in each corner and a chicken in the center of each side, and alternate the motifs in between. Make a row of dots 1-1/4" from the lower edge.

Space the dots 1-1/3" apart, and begin 1-3/4" from the corner.

Paint the hens' bodies and legs in gray, brushing unevenly to imitate feathers.

Work the color thicker in the center. Paint the hearts in a mixture of rose and blue. Paint the dots in blue gray and the hen's eye, comb, and wattle in rose.

Pin the checked strips of fabric end to end to form a ring. Using mitered corners, form the ring into a square with an inside measurement of 39" x 39". Form a similar square from the 4 strips of unbleached fabric. Press the seams open. Pin the checked border square to the unbleached border square, right sides together, and stitch together along outside edge. Turn right side out. Right sides together, pin large border square to painted tablecloth, and stitch together. Press seams. ■

TABLECLOTH WITH ROSES

PAGE 17

FINISHED MEASUREMENTS

58-1/2" x 58-1/2", motif about 18" x 18"

MATERIALS

60" x 60" light blue cotton fabric, tracing paper, stencilling paper or clear acetate, felt-tip pen, craft knife, masking tape, fabric paint in red, white (mix white and red to vary shades of pink), blue, green, and dark green,

stencilling brush, a piece of cardboard about 20" square, a piece of screening 20" square, an old toothbrush

INSTRUCTIONS

Hem the tablecloth by making a 1/2" hem with a 1/4" inner hem.

Using a photocopy machine, enlarge the rose motif to the size you want it. (The one pictured is 16" square.) Trace the rose motif onto tracing paper or a piece of stencilling paper. Pin the paper to the center of the cloth, and lightly pencil in the placement of the flowers.

With the felt-tip pen, trace the rose motif onto acetate or stencilling paper, creating a separate stencil for each color. It is only necessary to make one stencil for the small leaves and one for the repeated flower motifs. Cut out the stencils with craft knife.

Cut a circle about 16" in diameter from the middle of the cardboard, and

tape the screening over the hole. Hold the screen near the tablecloth, dip the toothbrush in paint, and rub the brush over the screen to spatter the cloth between the flower motifs. Spatter lightly in the center and more heavily at the outside edges (see the photo). Dip the stencil brush into fabric paint, then rub off excess paint on a paper towel until the brush is almost dry. Begin the corner motifs, then do the flowers, completing the largest and lightest areas first. After they are dry, paint the smaller and darker areas. ∎

BLACK AND GRAY TABLECLOTH

PAGES 18-19

FINISHED MEASUREMENTS

59" x 79-1/2"

MATERIALS

2-1/4 yds of gray cotton fabric 60" wide, fabric paint in black and transparent white (to mix with the black paint), a brush 3" wide, tailor's chalk, 8 yds of gray bias seam binding.

INSTRUCTIONS

With the tailor's chalk, mark 3" x 3" squares on fabric, beginning 2" from each edge. Mix the transparent white paint with a little black. Brush on the

squares, changing direction of brush strokes for each square. Don't try to paint evenly, but use photo as a guide. Try to vary the motif with light and dark squares.

Sew 1 edge of seam binding to wrong side of fabric, fold seam binding over tablecloth edge, and sew in place. ∎

TABLECLOTH WITH GRAPES

PAGE 20

MATERIALS

Closely woven cotton fabric in size desired, stencilling paper or clear acetate, felt-tip pen, craft knife, masking tape, fabric paint in purple, brown and 2 shades of green, 1/3" brush or sponge brush

INSTRUCTIONS

Use felt-tip pen to trace leaf pattern onto stencilling paper or acetate, and cut out leaf, taking some care to keep the cut-out piece intact. *Save the leaf cut-out.* To make the grape stencil, cut out a circle the appropriate size.

With a pencil, lightly mark the center of the cloth and the location of the motifs. Tape the leaf stencil to the fabric, and paint the cut-out area. Do not fill in completely.

Lightly sketch the shape of the grape bunch to use as a guide for placement of grapes. Overlap grapes as desired, using purple. Do not fill in stencil completely. When grapes are dry, add touches of brown to some of them.

Use leaf cut-out to form negative images of some of the leaves, using the second shade of green. Also use second green to highlight the edges of the filled-in leaves. ∎

Instructions continued on page 35.

TABLECLOTH WITH LEMONS

PAGE 21

FINISHED MEASUREMENTS

47-1/2" x 47-1/2"

MATERIALS

1-1/2 yds white cotton fabric with small green dots (or plain white cotton) 55" wide, stencilling paper or clear acetate, felt-tip pen, craft knife, masking tape, fabric paint in yellow, dark yellow, orange and green, stencilling brush, 3 yds turquoise zigzag rickrack. For accents: *either* embroidery floss in orange, green and light brown, or a narrow-tipped paint brush and light brown fabric paint.

INSTRUCTIONS

Cut 4 squares of fabric 26" x 26". Trace motifs onto stencilling paper or acetate, and cut out areas to be painted. Stencil the different fruit motifs onto the squares of fabric, positioning them where you like and taping the stencil to the fabric while you work. Mix the paints to get the desired colors, using orange or green for the shaded areas.

With embroidery: Embroider the stems in chain stitch with 1 strand of floss, using green for the oranges' stems and light brown for the lemons' stems. Embroider the shaded areas of the fruit in satin stitch, using 2 strands of orange floss.

Without embroidery: Using a narrow-tipped brush, paint the stems of the oranges green and the stems of the lemons light brown.

Right sides together, pin the 4 squares together to form a large square, and sew together with a 1/4" seam. On the right side of the cloth, sew rickrack over the seams. Make a 3/4" hem with mitered corners, and sew rickrack around the tablecloth 1" from the outside edge. ■

TABLECLOTH WITH CARS

PAGE 22

FINISHED MEASUREMENTS

Each motif is 4-1/2" x 9-1/2"

MATERIALS

White cotton fabric of desired shape and size, fabric paint in desired colors, stencilling paper or clear acetate, felt-tip pen, craft knife, pencil, masking tape, fabric paint, brush, seam binding to finish the edges

INSTRUCTIONS

Trace motif onto stencilling paper or acetate with felt-tip pen. With craft knife, cut out areas to be painted. Use the pencil to lightly mark the various positions of the motifs on the cloth. Tape stencil to cloth, and paint cut-out areas. (Put a piece of paper under the fabric when painting, in case the paint seeps through.) Each time, let the paint dry before removing the stencil.

To finish the hem, sew 1 edge of seam binding to wrong side of fabric, fold binding over tablecloth edge, and sew in place. ∎

Easter Egg Ensemble

PAGE 23

TABLECLOTH

MATERIALS

White cotton fabric to cover tabletop plus desired drop, stencilling paper or clear acetate, felt-tip pen, craft knife, masking tape, fabric paint in desired colors, stencilling brush

INSTRUCTIONS

On a piece of paper, draw your patterns for the eggs, making as many different styles as you like: horizontal and vertical stripes, for example. Leave some egg patterns plain, so you can decorate them free-hand later--for example, by adding polka dots. Draw a pattern for the grass (see the photo).

With a felt-tip pen, trace the patterns onto stencilling paper or clear acetate. Use the craft knife to cut out areas to be painted. Tape stencils to fabric, and paint bright colors with stencilling brush. When the tablecloth is dry, make a 1" hem with a 1/4" inner hem, or finish with bias binding.

EGG WARMER

MATERIALS

For each egg warmer: 6" x 9-3/4" white cotton fabric, felt of same size for lining, bias binding in light blue and green, fabric paint, stencilling brush

INSTRUCTIONS

Cut cotton into 2 squares 4" x 4". Paint on the eggs and the grass at the lower edge. On a 4" square piece of paper, draw a horseshoe-shaped pattern (for the egg warmer shape), and cut it out. Tape the pattern to the painted fabric, and cut out fabric, leaving 1/4" seam allowance. Cut out pieces of felt with the same pattern.

With right sides of cotton fabric together, sew together the curved portion of the egg warmer, leaving the bottom open. Turn right side out. Sew green bias binding to bottom edge and pale blue binding to the curved seam. Stitch felt pieces around curved sides, and insert liner into egg warmer.

TEA COZY

MATERIALS

1 yd white cotton fabric 55" wide, light blue and green bias binding, fiberfill, small amounts striped fabric, stencilling paper or clear acetate, craft knife, masking tape, fabric paint, stencilling brush

INSTRUCTIONS

Using the chart, make a paper pattern of the tea cozy. Pin to white fabric and cut out 2 pieces with a 1/4" seam allowance. Paint eggs and then grass on fabric. Cut a 4" x 38" strip from the white fabric for the panel. For the liner, cut out 4 pieces, using the paper pattern with 1/4" seam allowance but no hem. Cut 2 strips 4" x 32" for panels. From striped fabric cut out 1 strip 5-1/2" x 5-1/2".

Liner: Pin the panel between front and back pieces right sides together, and sew along rounded edges, leaving lower edge open. Make a second liner. Turn one liner right side out. Insert one liner inside the other, wrong sides together, and stuff with fiberfill. Fold in 1/4" at lower edge and sew in place.

Tea cozy: Pin the panel and the back and front pieces right sides together, and sew along rounded edges, leaving lower edge open. Sew light blue bias binding over the seams. Fold the striped fabric lengthwise, right sides facing. Sew lengthwise seam, leaving ends open. Turn right side out. Sew ends together and fold in half with seam at the center. Sew to center of center of panel, covering center of strip with seam binding to form bow. Insert liner in tea cozy. Fold hem to inside and sew over liner. Sew green seam binding over lower edge. ■

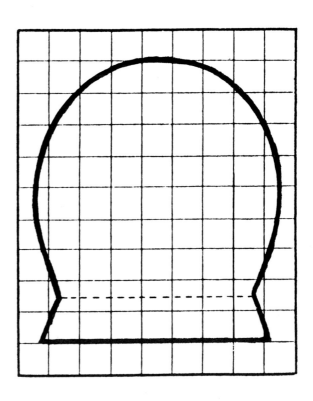

Breakfast Set

PAGE 24

FINISHED MEASUREMENTS

Tablecloth, 23" x 23"; napkins, 16" x 16"

MATERIALS

Fine weave cotton or linen fabric, stencilling paper or clear acetate, felt-tip pen, craft knife, masking tape, brush, fabric paint in red, white, yellow and green. *Optional:* DMC embroidery floss in salmon #948

INSTRUCTIONS

Cut the fabric 24" x 24" for tablecloth and 20" x 20" for each napkin. Sew a line of basting thread 2-1/4" from each edge to mark hem.

Enlarge motif to desired size. (The tablecloth motif is shown 7" square.) Trace motifs onto stencilling paper or clear acetate with felt-tip pen, and cut out areas to be painted. Place the stencil in corner, 1/2" from marked edge of tablecloth or 1/4" from marked edge of napkin. Tape stencil to fabric.

Brush red paint on the petals, brushing unevenly. Let dry completely, then brush over in white paint on the petals, to give a washed salmon look. Paint the centers in red. Outline the petals and the veins and make rays from the centers with red. Mix green and yellow paint and brush on leaves unevenly. Outline the leaves in yellow. Paint tendrils in yellow. (See photo.)

If you want to add optional embroidery, work a row of stem stitch from edge to edge on fabric, about 1-1/2" from each edge, using 2 strands of embroidery floss. Along the rows of stem stitch, run a piece of tape on fabric, then 1/3" inside the first tape, run a second tape. Paint a line of red between the tapes, let dry, then paint in white to form salmon stripe. Remove tape. Make a hem with mitered corners and sew in place with white sewing thread.

If you don't want to embroider, just place the tape by measuring 1-1/2" in from all edges. Then proceed with second tape and paint as directed. ■

Shown 66% of actual size. Photocopy at 152%.

TULIP NAPKINS

PAGE 25

FINISHED MEASUREMENTS
About 15" x 15"

MATERIALS
Ecru linen 16" x 16", paper, felt-tip pen, fabric paint in white, red and green, medium-width brushes, pencil. For accenting: *either* DMC embroidery floss in light pink #605, pink #956, green #913, yellow green #472; *or* narrow-tipped brushes for painting lines.

INSTRUCTIONS
The tulips aren't stenciled but are painted free-hand, for a more flowing effect. With a dark felt-tip pen, trace the motif on paper, then place the paper under the linen, so the sketch shows through. Position the motif in the upper right corner, about 2-1/4" from the top and side edges.

Mix red and white paint to make pink and paint the tulips, using the outlined motif as a guide and stroking lightly to give an uneven effect (see photo.) Mix green and white paint but not completely, to get a blended look, and paint the leaves.

With embroidery. With the pencil, draw the veins on the leaves and petals. With 2 strands of floss, embroider in stem stitch over the thick lines on the sketch and in outline stitch over the thin lines. Embroider the veins and the stem in stem stitch, using light green and green floss.

Also draw a line around the circumference of the napkin 1" from the edges. Using 2 strands of light pink or pink floss, embroider the border in chain stitch.

Make a 1/4" wide hem with a 1/8" inner hem and miter the corners. Sew in place with tiny stitches on wrong side of embroidery.

Without embroidery. Mix a darker pink paint, and paint in the accent lines on the tulips with a narrow-tipped brush. Mix a darker green, and paint in veins on the leaves. Stitch a 1/4" hem (with a 1/8" inner hem) by hand or by sewing machine. ■

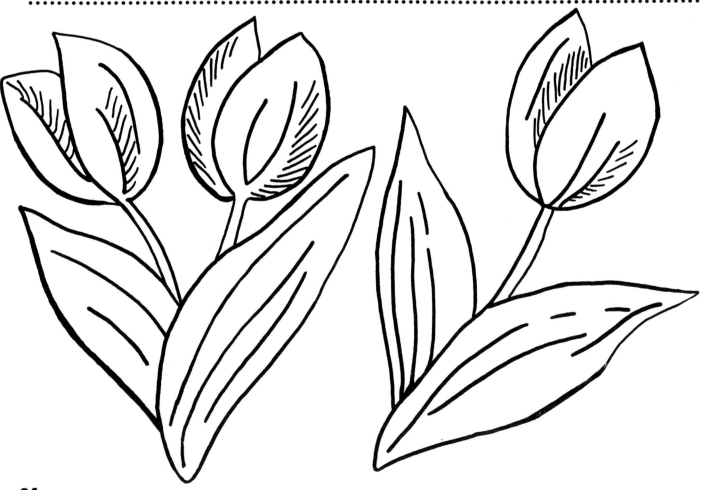

PLACE MATS
WITH SNOWMEN

PAGE 26

MATERIALS

Graph paper; paint and narrow-tipped brushes, or felt tip pens in various colors; glue, paper place mats and napkins

INSTRUCTIONS

Using the squares in the graph paper as your guide, paint snow people in appropriate colors. Cut out the completed figures, and glue them to brightly colored paper place mats and napkins. ■

Tablecloth with grapes (continued from page 28).

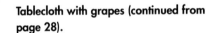

APPLIQUE

If you're looking for a quiet tablecloth, you'll have to look elsewhere. This one fairly shouts for joy. Machine stitching makes the project fast and easy. You'll need three shades of cotton fabric: light blue for the background, royal purple for the grapes, bright green for the leaves and stems. After copying the motifs onto tracing paper, cut out the appliques and pin them to the background fabric. Machine-stitch around them with a zigzag stitch, then sculpt the grapes and accent the leaves with more zigzagging.

INSTRUCTIONS FOR THIS PROJECT ARE FOUND ON PAGE 48.

APPLIQUE

To set an elegant Christmas table, start with a tablecloth in white and royal blue. You'll need white cotton fabric and two different blue-and-white prints. The cloth is scalloped around the hem, with appliqued Christmas balls that fit perfectly into the scalloped edges. Bows in light and medium blue finish the look.

INSTRUCTIONS FOR THIS PROJECT ARE FOUND ON PAGE 50.

APPLIQUE

T*his holiday tablecloth has it all—Christmas trees, stars, holly, even jingle bells that really jingle. The cloth consists of a red cotton circle with a row of zigzag stitching for a hem, and the cotton appliques are machine-stitched on. The bells hang from red ribbons looped through some oversized stitches of buttonhole thread.*

INSTRUCTIONS FOR THIS PROJECT ARE FOUND ON PAGE 51.

Applique

For poolside, lakeside, or just outside, this plastic tablecloth is waterproof, washable, and fun. You'll need a large piece of plastic for the background and small pieces in bright colors, prints, or stripes (why show any restraint at all?) for the appliques. Add a few gills and eyes, and you're ready for the great outdoors.

INSTRUCTIONS FOR THIS PROJECT
ARE FOUND ON PAGE 53.

APPLIQUE

T*his tablecloth offers so many choices it can paralyze the faint of heart. Choose a background fabric in any color you want, cut the patches from whatever fabrics you like in any shapes you please, machine-stitch them anywhere you desire, and embroider a few of them or not. Whatever.*

INSTRUCTIONS FOR THIS PROJECT
ARE FOUND ON PAGE 54.

APPLIQUE

Watermelon is a slice of summer, and this colorful cloth is just as lively as the season. The blue-and-white-checked fabric is the perfect background for the vibrant appliques, and the red bias-binding hem is exactly the right finishing touch.

INSTRUCTIONS FOR THIS PROJECT ARE FOUND ON PAGE 56.

APPLIQUE

Applique doesn't have to be saved for tablecloths. The technique also works well on smaller projects, like the coasters at left. They're simply pieces of background fabric with contrasting pieces zigzagged on, and with bias binding serving as hems and stems.

The tea cozy isn't quite as easy, but it too makes excellent use of applique, with fruit made from scraps of fabric and a basket made from bias seam binding. It's lined with fiberfill, to keep a teapot warm through a leisurely second cup.

INSTRUCTIONS FOR THIS PROJECT ARE FOUND ON PAGE 58.

APPLIQUE

These huge appliques are not as complicated to make as they might look. Each color started out as a simple square of fabric, which was folded and re-folded, then cut out along its edges through all layers. Although this one is done in brilliant colors and whimsical cut-out shapes, the concept lends itself to a variety of moods and treatments.

INSTRUCTIONS FOR THIS PROJECT ARE FOUND ON PAGE 62.

APPLIQUE

*T*he Christmas season brings out the traditionalist in all of us, and this tablecloth is as traditional as they come: appliqued with a time-honored quilt pattern in red and green.

Each applique consists of eight diamonds cut from various calicos and machine-stitched in place to form a star. The bright red cloth is hemmed with long strips of calico, much the same way you'd apply bias binding.

INSTRUCTIONS FOR THIS PROJECT ARE FOUND ON PAGE 63.

Tablecloth with Grapes

PAGES 36-37

FINISHED MEASUREMENTS

34-3/4" x 44"

MATERIALS

1-1/4 yds light blue cotton fabric 36" wide, 3/4 yd purple cotton fabric 36" wide, 3/4 yd green cotton 36" wide, fusible interfacing, DMC cotton sewing thread in green ombre and purple ombre, tracing paper, dressmaker's carbon, scissors with a sharp point, a clear marker.

INSTRUCTIONS

Each motif wraps around a corner of the tablecloth, with the long side of the motif on the long side of the cloth. Enlarge the pattern so the long side measures 22" from the tip of the bottom grape to the tip of the end leaf. (The long sides are shown in the photo.) The short side should measure 17".

Trace the applique on tracing paper; turn it over to reverse the motif and

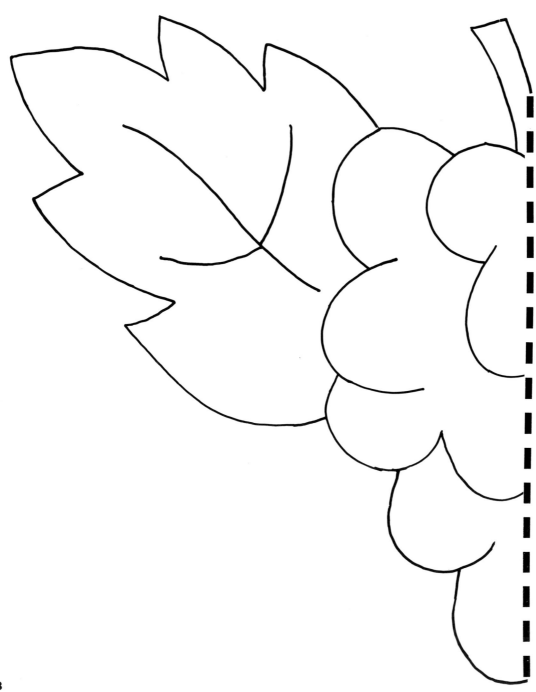

trace another motif. With the clear marker, mark the center of the light blue cotton fabric and mark the corners so that the piece measures 34-3/4" x 44". Mark the horizontal and vertical center of each corner. Pin interfacing to purple and green fabric. Tape the tracing paper over the purple and green fabric and cut out both motifs through double thicknesses to produce 4 motifs. Cut the grapes out of the purple fabric and the leaves out of the green fabric. Allow 1/4" seam allowance around leaves. Pin the motifs to the blue fabric: first the leaves, then the grapes overlapping the leaves. The grapes should be slightly inside the blue fabric corner. Place the stem under the grapes. With carbon, mark the edges on the fabric. With sewing machine, zigzag stitch inside the motifs as shown on photo. Cut away excess blue fabric taking care not to cut any threads of the zigzag stitches. ■

Join pattern at dotted line (as shown in box) and enlarge as per directions.

CHRISTMAS TABLECLOTH WITH BLUE BALLS

PAGE 38

FINISHED MEASUREMENTS

Each ball is 4-3/4" in diameter.

MATERIALS

White cotton fabric, 2 kinds of blue and white print fabric, white and blue thread, white Velcro, dark and light blue ribbon 1/2" wide, fusible interfacing, tracing paper, white paper, basting thread, cardboard, pencil with sharp point, hobby glue.

Note: To determine amount of fabric needed measure the tabletop, add 14" overhang on all sides plus hem. Allow for an uneven number of Christmas balls between corners. Each corner motif is about 11-3/4" wide, each scallop is about 4" wide.

INSTRUCTIONS

Enlarge the pattern so that the ball is 4-3/4" in diameter. Trace the corner motif on a piece of cardboard. Allowing 1-1/2" all around, trace the corner motif in each corner of the cloth, then trace the scallops all around the edges, placing the first ball motif about 11-3/4" from the corner. Adjust the size of the scallops as necessary so that the last ball on each side is equally spaced from the corners. Cut out around traced edges.

With pins, mark positions for Christmas balls. Plan on having the same design in opposite corners and alternate designs. With white sewing thread, zigzag stitch along all the scalloped edges (not including ball edges). Tip: make the pattern on tracing paper, pin to the fabric and sew through the paper to keep the scallop even.

Christmas balls: Using the pattern for the ball, cut out fabric for Christmas balls. Pin fabric and interfacing together and position on tablecloth. Be sure the edges of the fabric exactly match the curve of the scallops and are held securely in place. With blue sewing thread, zigzag stitch all around edges. Cut the excess material on the lower edge of the scallops, taking care not to clip threads.

Make a bow for each Christmas ball. Cut a piece of light blue ribbon about 2-1/4" long. Cut blue ribbon in 13-3/4" strips. Fold in half with ends at center, then make 2 loops from each half and tack all ends of loops at center. Cover with the light blue ribbon. Tack in place at back of bow. Cut 3-1/2" long strips of dark blue ribbon and cut ends as shown in photo. Fold in half and sew to back of bow as shown in photo. Cut small pieces of Velcro and put the soft piece above each ball and the rough piece on the back of each bow. Attach bows to tablecloth. ■

• •

Shown 47% of actual size.
Photocopy at 213%.

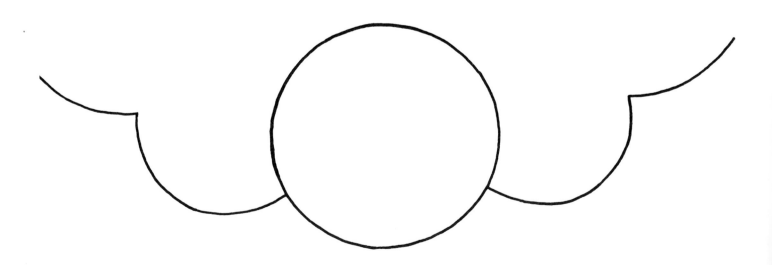

TABLECLOTH WITH CHRISTMAS MOTIFS

PAGE 39

FINISHED MEASUREMENTS

55" diameter

MATERIALS

A round red tablecloth 55" in diameter or 2 yds of red cotton fabric 60" wide, black and red sewing machine thread, red buttonhole thread, pieces of white, green and yellow cotton fabric, fusible interfacing, tracing paper, dressmaker's carbon, basting thread, 11 yds of 1-1/4" wide red ribbon, 40 metal jingle bells, a piece of cardboard 3/4" x 2". Note: The little balls tied around the edges of the tablecloth can be removed for washing.

INSTRUCTIONS

Cut a circle from red fabric about 56" in diameter. Zigzag a hem 1/4" wide.

Trace the motifs on tracing paper. Pin to fabric and fusible interfacing and cut out. Cut out 8 Christmas trees and 9 holly leaves from green fabric. Cut out 8 small stars, 6 large stars and 18 berries from white fabric. Cut out 8 pots and 6 large stars from yellow fabric. (Cut out all pieces without seam allowances.)

Place 1 holly leaf in the middle of the cloth. About 12" from the center, make a circle of motifs, alternating 4 Christmas trees, 2 white and 2 yellow stars. About 4" below make another circle of motifs of Christmas trees, holly, 2 yellow and 2 white stars. Leave about 8" to 10" between motifs. Each holly leaf should be centered between a star and a tree. See photo. Zigzag motifs to fabric, working a zigzag line between the berries of the holly and between the pot and the tree.

1/4" from the hem, make a pair of stitches using the buttonhole thread through which you thread the ribbon for the bells. Separate each pair by about 4-1/4" (you'll need 40 bells). Cut 40 pieces of red ribbon about 10" long. Thread the ribbon through the stitches and attach a bell. Use the cardboard to measure the distance from the bow so that all bells are evenly spaced around tablecloth. ∎

Pattern continued on next page.

Pattern continued from previous page.

TABLECLOTH WITH FISH

PAGE 40

FINISHED MEASUREMENTS

60" x 60"

MATERIALS

For the background: a piece of plastic 60" x 60". For the appliques: striped, patterned or solid color plastic, matching sewing machine thread, tape.

INSTRUCTIONS

Using the chart, make a pattern. (Each square equals 1-1/2".) Cut the gill lines and eye motifs separately, and cut out the complete fish. Tape patterns to plastic and cut out pieces without seam allowances. Flip the pattern over to make fish face either way. With zigzag stitch, applique the eye and gill lines to the fish using the photo as a guide. Tape the pieces to the plastic background as you desire and machine applique using matching thread. Cut a scallop edge around the tablecloth. ■

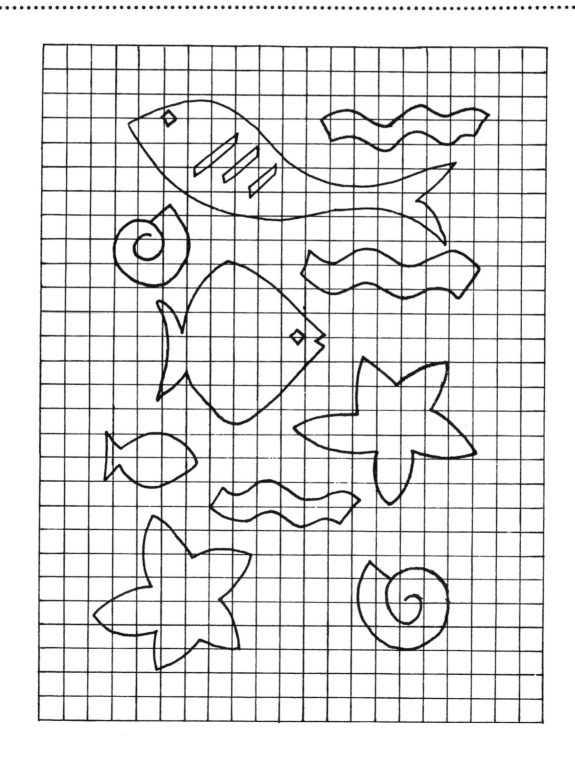

Tablecloth
with Patches

PAGE 41

FINISHED MEASUREMENTS

41-1/2" x 41-1/2"

MATERIALS

White cotton fabric 40" x 40". For the appliques, use different color fabric. Embroidery floss, sewing thread, 4 strips of fabric 3-1/4" x 44".

INSTRUCTIONS

Cut patches of fabric in any size and shape you desire. If desired, embroider some of the motifs on some of the patches in stem stitch and padded satin stitch using 4 strands of embroidery floss.

Arrange the patches on the white cotton fabric, using the photo as a guide. Applique the patches using zigzag stitch.

With right sides together, sew the strips to the edges by centering them. Cut the corners diagonally so as to sew mitered corners. Hem the strips. ■

WATERMELON TABLECLOTH

PAGE 42

FINISHED MEASUREMENTS

53-1/4" x 53-1/4"

MATERIALS

Blue and white checked cotton fabric 54" x 54", 2-1/4 yds red bias tape 3/4" wide, red fabric 13-3/4" x 35-1/2", green fabric 20" x 35-1/2", white fabric 23-3/4" x 35-1/2", matching sewing thread, black sewing machine thread, fusible interfacing.

INSTRUCTIONS

Line all the fabric to be appliqued with interfacing. Trace the motifs on tracing paper with each block 1-1/4" x 1-1/4". Cut out 24 white background pieces. Cut out 24 red and green pieces. Sew bias tape to wrong side of tablecloth edges, fold over to right side and sew in place, allowing enough material at each corner to make a mitered corner. Sew on appliques using the sketch as a guide beginning in 1 corner. Turn sketch and continue around entire tablecloth. Use your imagination for placement of the slices. Using zigzag stitch, machine embroider seeds, varying their size, shape and placement. ■

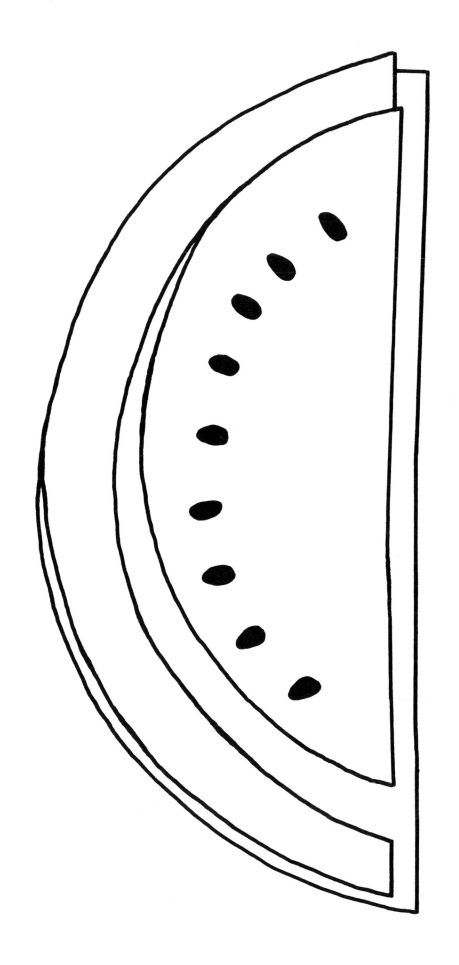

Tea Cozy
with Fruit

PAGE 43

FINISHED MEASUREMENTS

12-1/2" x 15-3/4"

MATERIALS

3/4 yd of soft green striped cotton fabric 36" wide. *For the lining:* 1-1/2 yd soft green cotton fabric 36" wide. Fiberfill. *For the appliques:* small amounts of light pink, light yellow, light orange, light green and lilac cotton fabric. Matching sewing machine thread. Fusible interfacing. 1-1/2 yd of light brown bias seam binding. Small amounts of lilac, green and orange bias seam binding. Tracing paper and dressmaker's carbon.

INSTRUCTIONS

Using the sketch, make a paper pattern on tracing paper with each square 1-1/2" x 1-1/2". Pin to 1 piece of striped fabric with 1-1/4" seam allowance and a hem allowance of 2".

Appliques: Trace the appliqued motifs onto tracing paper, and transfer design onto pieces of fabric. Pin fusible interfacing to fabric. Cut out the whole apple and pear without a seam allowance. Cut out an apple of every color except light yellow. Cut out a pear of every color. Cut the leaves from light green. Center the fruit motifs 1-1/4" from lower edge (above 2" hem line). Use the photo as a guide for placement. Zigzag stitch using matching color thread. Sew on the top apples first. Sew on leaves last.

Fruit basket: Fold the seam binding in half. Cut 5 strips of seam binding twice the height of the basket. Beginning at left edge, pin a piece of seam binding as shown in sketch. With second half of strip, make a V. 1-1/4" from lower point of V, pin a second V, overlapping the second V over the second half of the first strip. Continue

with the 5 strips, ending with right side of basket. Pin 2 short pieces under the side seams at upper corners. Sew strips in place. Pin the top and lower strips in place and sew in place.

Cut out back of tea cozy allowing 1/4" seam allowance and hem same as front. Cut out 2 strips 3-1/4" x 19-3/4" for panel. Cut out 6 pieces of soft green fabric for lining with 1/4" seam allowance and with 1/8" seam allowance for hem. Cut out 6 strips for panel 3-1/4" x 18-1/2". Cut out 3-1/4" lengths of remaining pieces of seam binding. Fold each piece in half and braid together. Sew ends to each edge of right side of center of panel. With right sides together, pin the center panel to the front and the back of outside of tea cozy. Sew together. Turn right side out.

From lining material, make 3 inner tea cozies. Pin the panel pieces to the back and front and sew around. Place 1 lining inside the outside piece, wrong sides together and fold the hem of the outside piece and sew in place. Place the 2 remaining pieces, wrong sides together. Stuff with fiberfill and fold in lower edges and sew seam. Place lining inside tea cozy. ■

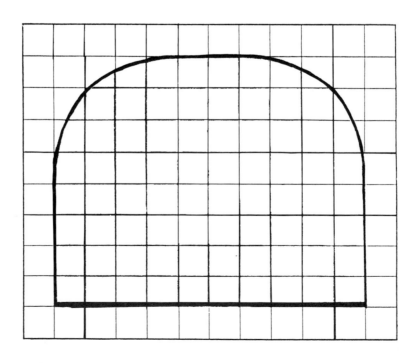

FRUIT COASTERS

FINISHED MEASUREMENTS

About 4-1/2" x 5"

MATERIALS

Each apple coaster: a piece of red cotton fabric about 6" x 12", small amounts of orange, yellow, light green and green cotton fabric, about 27-1/2" green bias seam binding, fusible interfacing, sewing thread in matching colors. *Each melon coaster:* light green cotton fabric 6" x 12", small amount of green cotton fabric, 20" of green bias tape, fusible interfacing, green sewing thread.

INSTRUCTIONS

Line the pieces of cotton with fusible interfacing. Trace the outlines of the coasters on tracing paper, then cut out pieces of cotton fabric, using key as a guide to colors. Cut out base pieces using double thickness of red or green fabric. Cut out other pieces without seam allowances. Place the 2 base pieces wrong sides together and zigzag around edges. Zigzag the other pieces to the top of the underpieces.

Sew the green bias tape around the edges of the base pieces. For stem, take a piece of bias tape 2-1/2" long and double it. Sew through all thicknesses and sew to top of melon. Sew bias tape around the leaf, leaving an end folded over for stem, and sew to base. ■

KEY TO SKETCH OF COASTERS
1 = red
2 = orange
3 = yellow
4 = light green
5 = green

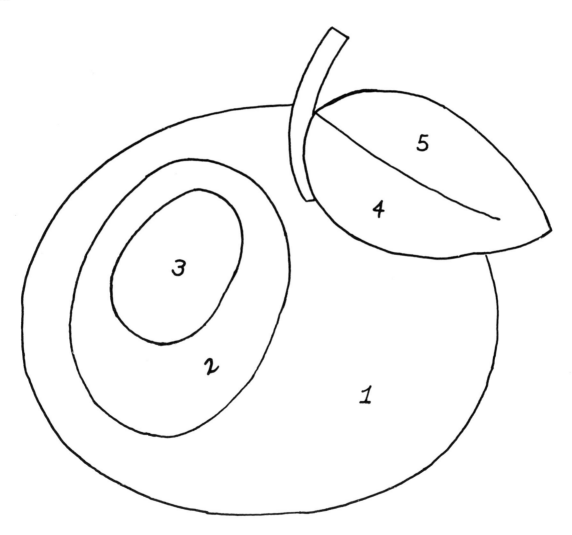

Red and Yellow Applique

PAGES 44-45

FINISHED MEASUREMENTS

59" x 84-3/4"

MATERIALS

2-1/2 yds of red cotton fabric 60" wide, 1 yd yellow cotton 60" wide, 2 yds green cotton fabric 36" wide, yellow and green sewing machine thread, 8 yds yellow bias seam binding 3/4" wide, tracing graph paper with 1-1/2" 1-1/2" squares, sharp scissors.

INSTRUCTIONS

Using the graph paper make full-size paper patterns. Cut 2 pieces of green cotton 36" x 36". Cut these squares diagonally to form 4 triangles. Fold 1 triangle diagonally and pin on the pattern. Cut out motifs along folded edge and side edges. Unfold and press. Pin the green applique onto the end of the red cloth and machine applique in place. Cut a 37-1/2" x 37-1/2" square of yel-

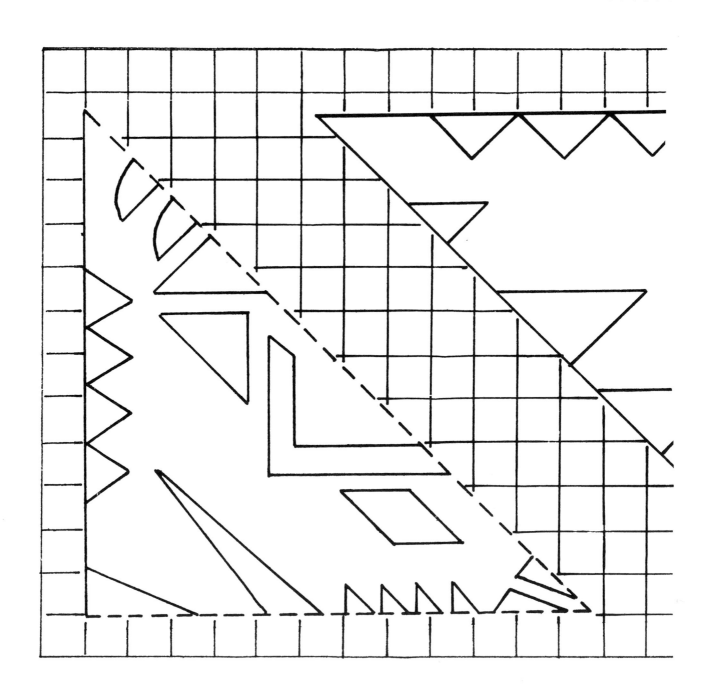

low cotton. Fold the fabric in half so you have an 18-3/4" x 18-3/4" square. Fold the folded edge to meet the open end. Pin on the center pattern and cut out the motifs. If the fabric is too thick to cut through, cut each half separately. Unfold and press. Pin the yellow applique to the center of the red cloth and machine applique in place.

Along one short end of the tablecloth, sew on seam binding. Pin the seam binding to the wrong side of the tablecloth and sew in place. Fold the seam binding to right side and sew in place. Continue all around the cloth, overlapping the ends. ■

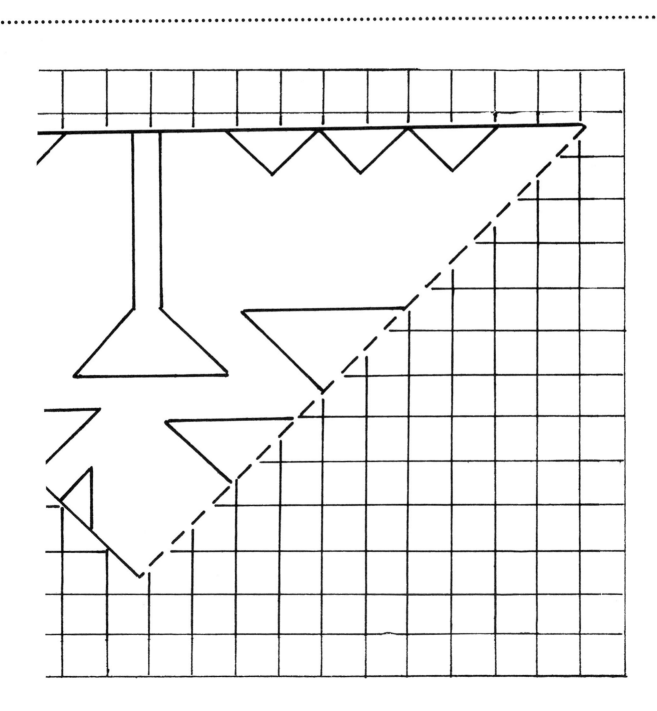

CHRISTMAS STAR TABLECLOTH

PAGES 46-47

FINISHED MEASUREMENTS

Each appliqued star 7-1/2" x 7-1/2", tablecloth 59" x 72-3/4".

MATERIALS

2 yds red and white dotted cotton fabric 60" wide, calico fabric with different designs for the stars, green and red sewing thread, fusible interfacing, tracing paper, basting thread, cardboard paper, pencil with a sharp point, glue, scissors.

Note: The instructions are for a tabletop 31-1/2" x 47-1/4". You can adapt the instructions for any size.

INSTRUCTIONS

Trim the fabric to exact measurements of 59" x 72-3/4". Mark the horizontal and vertical center. Trace the pattern of the diamond on cardboard and cut out. Tip: You may cut out a half pattern and place on folded fabric so that both sides are exactly the same.

Trace diamonds onto fabrics, and cut out. Iron fusible interfacing to wrong side of diamonds and arrange in stars on tablecloth. Place 9 stars on each long side and 5 stars on each narrow side. Place stars over the center 30" of long sides and 22-1/2" of narrow sides. The lower edge of each star should be 3" from lower edge of fabric. Use 8 diamonds for each star, staggering the designs on the fabric. You will have a total of 28 stars on the fabric. Use a sewing machine and green thread to zigzag around edges and between diamonds.

For hem, cut out strips of calico 2" wide and desired length. Place strips right sides together and sew together with 1/4" seams. Two strips should be 59-1/2" long and 2 strips should be 74-1/2" long. Press open. With right sides facing, place the long strips on the long side and sew to tablecloth edge, making a 1/4" seam. Fold in half to inside and hem stitch in place. Work the long sides first, then work the short sides to cover the long side hems. ■

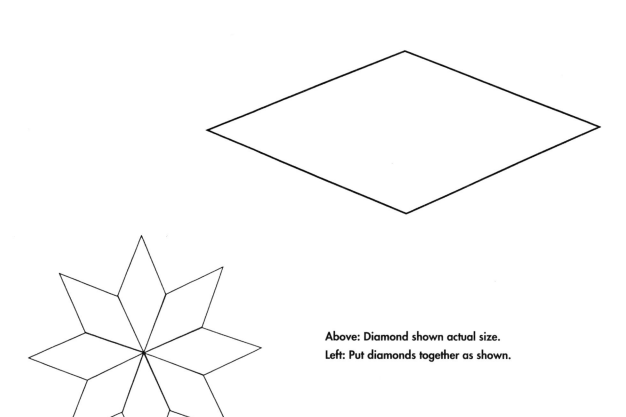

Above: Diamond shown actual size.
Left: Put diamonds together as shown.

SEWING

This huge white bow gets its body from spray starch and its shine from the cellophane wrapped around it. It's pinned onto the tablecloth with corsage pins, which hold the hand-gathered tablecloth in place.

Instructions for this project
are found on page 81.

SEWING

*T*his sunny table setting promises good food and good cheer. The yellow cotton tablecloth underneath is merely hemmed. The chintz one on top is gathered at the edges, so that it drapes gracefully. The tea cozy in matching chintz keeps things warm, and the bread napkin echoes the color scheme in cross stitch.

INSTRUCTIONS FOR THE TABLECLOTH AND TEA COZY ARE FOUND ON PAGES 81 AND 82. INSTRUCTIONS FOR THE BREAD NAPKIN ARE FOUND ON PAGE 143.

SEWING

For a wedding table as joyous as the occasion, dress up a plain white tablecloth with an oversize ruffle and pink fabric roses. As impressive as they look, the decorations don't demand a lot of work: just some machine stitching, a little gathering, a little rolling of fabric, and a bit of hand tacking.

INSTRUCTIONS FOR THIS PROJECT ARE FOUND ON PAGE 82.

SEWING

*I*t's not really summer until you dine outdoors. With a padded picnic cloth, you'll be both comfortable and well fed. Cut a piece of gaily striped cotton fabric into squares and sew them back together, alternating the direction of the stripes. Line the cloth with a solid color, stuff it with fiberfill batting, and settle down for a fine summer afternoon.

INSTRUCTIONS FOR THIS PROJECT ARE FOUND ON PAGE 83.

SEWING

elow: A picnic becomes an occasion when you bring a padded picnic cloth and a basket lined in the same fabric. The picnic cloth is padded with fiberfill batting, and the basket liner is attached with double-sided tape or hobby glue.

Right: A simple tablecloth becomes festive with huge pink bows attached to the corners. Vary the fabric for the tablecloth and the color of the bows to suit the setting.

INSTRUCTIONS FOR THIS PROJECT ARE FOUND ON PAGE 84.

SEWING

W*hen you find a fabric you really like, make the most of it. This coordinated table setting pairs a tablecloth with all kinds of accessories. The tablecloth has gathered sides, for a little extra zing. The well-shaped liner for the bread basket has a dark green border and iron-on appliques. The curved border of the place mats contrasts nicely with the straight-lined fabric. And the napkins boast ruffled borders and easy appliques.*

INSTRUCTIONS FOR THIS PROJECT ARE FOUND ON PAGE 85.

SEWING

F*or a festive Christmas table, make two tablecloths in holiday colors. Place the first tablecloth over the table in the conventional way, then place the second so that its corners fall on the sides of the table. As a final touch, wrap small boxes or blocks of plastic foam in Christmas wrapping paper, and hang them from ribbons at the corners of the table.*

INSTRUCTIONS FOR THIS PROJECT
ARE FOUND ON PAGE 87.

Decorating a tablecloth with "stiffy bows" is an English idea that's well worth borrowing. The bows are strips of fabric painted with white glue thinned with water. The damp strips of fabric are shaped into a bow, then propped in place with paper towel rollers until dry.

INSTRUCTIONS FOR THIS PROJECT
ARE FOUND ON PAGE 87.

SEWING

O n this table linen, the ribbons lie in channels created for them. *Threads have been pulled from the fabric in one direction— horizontal threads for horizontal ribbons, vertical threads for vertical ribbons. The ribbons are then pulled over and under the cross threads, which hold them in place.*

INSTRUCTIONS FOR THIS PROJECT
ARE FOUND ON PAGE 89.

SEWING

B *ecause ribbons come in various widths and an array of colors, you can create dozens of different place mats, tablecloths, table runners, and napkins using the same technique.*

INSTRUCTIONS FOR THIS PROJECT ARE FOUND ON PAGE 90.

TABLECLOTH WITH SHINY BOW

PAGE 65

FINISHED MEASUREMENTS

Each hanging bow is about 13-3/4" x 17-3/4". Tabletop bow 4" x 17-3/4".

MATERIALS

White fabric of cotton, damask or chintz, starch, white sewing thread, transparent cellophane (available in sheets at the stationery store), double-sided tape, long corsage pins.

Note: Measure the tabletop and add 20" for overhang at each end and side and 20" for the draped ruffle on each side. Also allow 1-1/2" for hem.

INSTRUCTIONS

Cut out fabric and make a 1" hem (1/2" inner hem) with mitered corners all around.

Cut out a bow of white fabric: 1 strip 5-1/2" x 21-3/4" for the loops and a piece 5-1/2" x 25-1/2" for the tie and ends of the bow. Cut a piece of cellophane 5-1/2" x 21-3/4". Spray starch on both sides of fabric strips and fold long sides together to meet at center forming strips 2-3/4" wide. Fold the strip of cellophane around the short strip and tape the long edges together. Fold the long ends so that the narrow ends slightly overlap at the center, and tack the ends in place. Fold the long strip in half and fold over the center of the looped strip, gathering slightly. Tack at back of bow (see photo).

Place the tablecloth on the table. Gather the sides at corners and at center, and pin with corsage pins. Pin bows to each gather. ■

GATHERED TABLECLOTH

PAGES 66-67

MATERIALS

47" wide yellow chintz, yellow cotton fabric 55" wide, 1" wide twill tape, cotton cord, matching sewing thread, heavy paper, darning needle.

Note: Measure the length and width of the table. Allow for desired overhang, plus 1-1/2" hem. For the top tablecloth, add 17" to tabletop measurements including 1-1/4" hem for each side of overhang. This extra material will be gathered as shown in photo.

INSTRUCTIONS

Yellow tablecloth: Make a hem 1-1/4" wide with a 1/4" inner hem.

Chintz tablecloth: Cut out a square of heavy paper 15-3/4" x 15-3/4". Draw a quarter circle from 1 corner to opposite corner. Pin or tape pattern to fabric, and use pattern to cut out round corners on fabric. Make a 3/4" hem with 1/2" inner hem around all edges. Cut 16 pieces 11" long of twill tape and sew 1 piece to center of each corner, sewing along each long edge and at center to form channels. Thread cord through channels. Sew more channels 12" from each corner center and space along sides as desired. Thread cord through channels, gather as desired and knot cords.

TEA COZY

FINISHED MEASUREMENTS

11-3/4" x 15"

MATERIALS

1/4 yd striped/flowered fabric 55" wide, striped fabric 10" x 18". Center panel: striped fabric 3-1/4" x 34-1/2". 22" of 1" wide twill tape, 1-1/2 yds of cotton cord, heavy paper, matching sewing thread. Lining: 1/2 yd light blue cotton 55" wide. Fiberfill batting.

INSTRUCTIONS

Make a paper pattern using the chart as a guide. Each square equals 1-1/2" x 1-1/2". Pin the pattern to striped/flowered fabric (front) and striped fabric (back). Cut out pieces so that the stripe of the back matches the center stripe of front, allowing 1/4" seam allowance and 3/4" hem allowance on lower edge of back. Allow an extra 8" at the lower edge of the front.

Fold the blue lining material so that the selvedge edges meet at the center. Cut out 4 pieces using the pattern piece allowing 1/4" seam allowance. Using the pattern piece, cut out 2 pieces of fiberfill batting without seam allowance. Cut the twill tape into 2 equal length pieces, each piece 11" long. Sew to wrong side of lower edge of front beginning 1-1/4" from lower edge and 4-1/4" from side seam. Sew along both long edges and down the center to form channels. Thread in cotton cord and gather so that the ruffle is 4" wide. Pin the striped panel to the back and sew in place. Pin the panel to the front, gathering the ruffle to fit. See photo. Turn right side out and fold in lower 1/4" for hem. Sew in place.

Lining: With right sides together, sew panel to 1 piece of lining, then sew to second piece to make 1 lining. Make a second lining. Tack fiberfill batting to wrong side of 1 lining. Turn second lining right side out and insert lined piece to second piece. Hem lower edge. Insert in outside piece of tea cozy. ■

Continued from previous page.

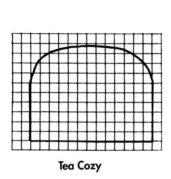

Tea Cozy

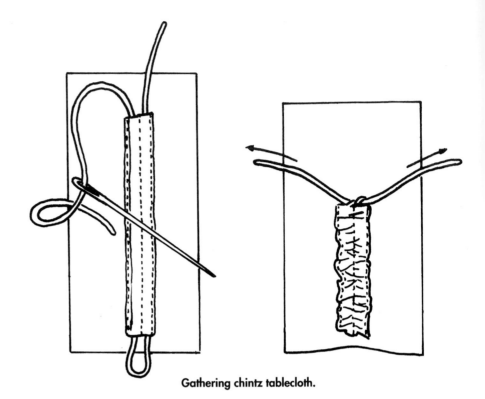

Gathering chintz tablecloth.

WEDDING TABLECLOTH

PAGES 68-69

MATERIALS

White, pink and light green fabric, paper, matching sewing thread, a white tablecloth, fiberfill.

INSTRUCTIONS

Cut a strip of white fabric 25-1/2" wide. Allow 1-1/2 times the total desired length. With right sides together, sew the narrow ends together to form ring. Fold the fabric right sides together and sew together, leaving a 12" opening at center. Turn right side out and sew opening closed. Fold fabric so that seam is in the center of the strip. Run a line of basting thread along the center of the strip. Gather the strip to desired length. Sew the ruffle to the table as shown in photo.

From pink fabric, make a strip 7" x 29-1/2" for each rose. With right sides together, fold the strip in half. Sew along the long side, leaving an opening at center. Turn right side out and sew the opening closed. 1/4" from the seam edge, run a line of basting stitches. Roll the fabric into a rose shape and gather the strip for desired effect.

For each leaf, cut 2 strips of green fabric about 4-3/4" long x 2-1/2" wide plus 1/4" seam allowance. Make a point on 1 narrow end and a straight edge at the other. With right sides together, sew around leaf, leaving straight edge open. Turn right side out, stuff lightly with fiberfill, and sew lower seam. Sew 1 rose and 2 leaves at desired intervals on ruffle. ■

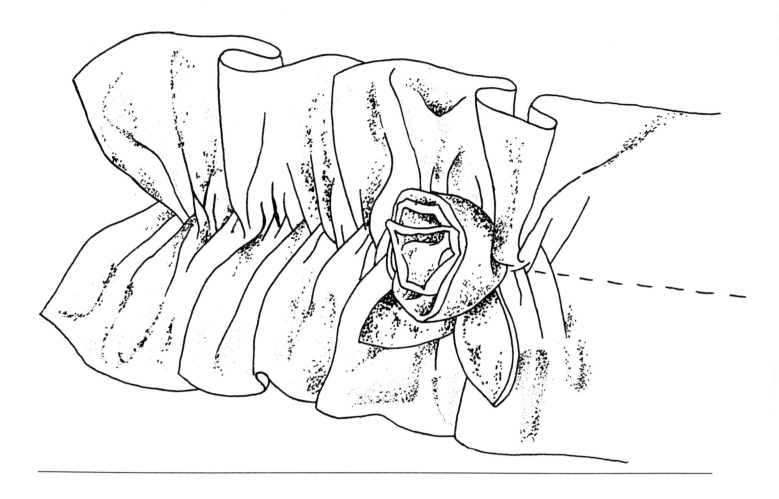

PICNIC CLOTH

PAGES 70-71

FINISHED MEASUREMENTS

59" x 59"

MATERIALS

1-3/4 yds striped cotton fabric 60" wide, 2-1/4 yds blue cotton fabric 60" wide, fiberfill batting.

INSTRUCTIONS

Cut out striped blocks 18-1/2" x 18-1/2". Cut a piece of blue fabric 54" x 54" and a strip 5-1/2" x 59". Cut a piece of fiberfill 58" x 58".

For the top: Lay the striped blocks 3 across and 3 down with the direction of the stripes alternating. With right sides together, sew the blocks together with 1/4" seam allowance. With right sides together, sew on the strip of blue material to the top, folding the fabric at the corners to form right angles. The top piece now measures 54" x 54". With right sides together, pin the blue fabric and the top together and sew around 3 sides, leaving the last side open. Trim corners and turn right side out. Stuff batting in open side and pin in place. Sew the last side closed. Sew around the edges of the striped piece and the blue strip through all thicknesses to hold the batting in place. ■

Picnic Cloth and Basket Liner

PAGE 72

BASKET LINER

FINISHED MEASUREMENTS

Basket 36" deep, 15-3/4" wide and 6" high.

MATERIALS

1 yd of printed cotton fabric 60" wide, fusible interfacing, elastic 1" wide, sewing machine thread, double sided tape or hobby glue.

INSTRUCTIONS

Cut a piece of fabric 18-1/2" x 23-3/4" to line basket. Cut a piece 13-3/4" x 19" to line lid. For the pocket, cut a strip 6- 1/4" x 21-3/4". To cover the elastic, cut 3 strips 3-1/4" x 6". Cut 1 strip 3-1/4" x 52-3/4" for the lid and 1 strip 3-1/4" x 51-1/4" for the basket.

Cut 1-1/4" diagonal lines in each corner of the lid fabric, and cut 3-1/2" diagonal lines in each corner of the basket fabric. Hem each side of the lid, basket and pocket fabric with a 1/4" hem.

For the pocket, make a 1-1/4" hem on 1 long side with a 1/4" inner hem, leaving the ends open. Thread in a piece of 15-3/4" elastic in the hem and tack ends in place. Fold 1/4" of side and lower edges to wrong side and sew in place. Gather the lower edge of the pocket and pin so that the entire length is 15-3/4". Sew the pocket to the lid lining, matching side seams and beginning 1-1/2" from the lower edge. Sew the pocket in place. Make 2 vertical seams to form pockets. (See photo.)

Fold the small strips right sides together and sew along long edges to form 1-1/4" channels. Do not sew ends. Turn right side out. Cut 2-1/2" long strips of elastic and insert in fabric channels. Tack ends. Sew ends to form ring and sew to lid as shown in photo. Place fabric in lid, folding the cut edges of the corners to sides of basket and tack in place.

Side linings: Sew narrow ends of the strips to form rings. Turn 3/4" at lower and upper edges to inside and press in place so that the strip is 1-3/4" wide.

Glue or tape with double sided tape to sides of lid and basket.

PICNIC CLOTH

FINISHED MEASUREMENTS

35-1/2" x 49-1/4"

MATERIALS

2-1/2 yds of printed cotton fabric 60" wide, fiberfill batting about 35-1/2" x 49-1/2", basting thread.

INSTRUCTIONS

Cut a piece of fabric 45" x 59" and a piece 29" x 43". On the larger piece, fold 3/4" to wrong side. Place this piece on a table with wrong side facing up. Lay batting over it and cut, leaving 4" of fabric uncovered all around. Place the smaller piece of fabric with wrong side against the batting; the top piece will be about 3-1/4" smaller all around than the fiberfill. Fold the corners of the larger piece to the corners of the top piece, overlapping by 3/4", and pin in place. Now fold 4" of all the edges of larger piece to smaller piece. Make mitered corners and sew corners by hand. Make an inner hem on larger piece and sew to smaller piece. ∎

Tablecloth with Corner Bows

PAGE 73

FINISHED MEASUREMENTS

74-3/4" x 90-1/2"

MATERIALS

4-1/2 yds of chintz fabric about 45" wide, 1-1/2 yds pink cotton fabric 60" wide, white and pink sewing thread.

INSTRUCTIONS

Cut the chintz fabric into 2 pieces about 47" x 80", being sure that the stripes will match when sewn together. Cut the pink cotton into 4 pieces 13-1/2" x 60" and 4 strips 1-1/4" x 4".

Place the 2 pieces of chintz right sides together and make a 1/4" seam. Make a 1" hem along all edges with mitered corners.

Place 2 pink strips right sides together and sew along 3 sides with a 1/4" seam allowance. Trim seam allowances and turn right side out. Sew the open end. Make a 2nd piece and sew smaller strips in the same way with a 1/8" seam allowance. Sew the narrow ends into a ring.

Place the tablecloth on the table and mark positions of corners. Sew the small strips diagonally to the corners to form loops. Thread the long strips through the loops and tie a bow. ∎

GREEN STRIPED TABLECLOTH AND ACCESSORIES

PAGES 74-75

TABLECLOTH

MATERIALS

3-1/4 yds green/white striped fabric 60" wide, sewing machine thread.

Note: This tablecloth was made for a table 31-1/2" x 47-1/4". You may adapt the instructions for any size table.

INSTRUCTIONS

Cut a piece of fabric 32-1/4" x 48" with the long stripe along the long edge. Cut 4 strips 14-1/2" x 59" and 4 strips 14-1/2" x 21-3/4" with the long stripe along the short edge. Sew the narrow ends of the strips together, alternating a long strip with a short strip. At one edge make a 1/4" hem with 1/4" inner hem. Run 2 basting threads along the other edge and gather to a total diameter of 4-1/4 yds around. Pin the ruffle to the top piece, right sides together, adjusting the gathers as you go. Sew all around.

BREAD BASKET NAPKIN

FINISHED MEASUREMENTS

30" x 30"

MATERIALS

20-1/2" x 20-1/2" of white cotton fabric, 1/3 yd of green fabric 36" wide, sewing machine thread. For the appliques: small amount of light green and green cotton fabric, iron-on fusible web, green felt-tip fabric marker.

Note: For the longest lasting results, the appliques can all be sewn on with zigzag stitch. Fusible web resembles fusible interfacing, except the former bonds on *both* sides and thus can be used to bond appliques to background fabric quickly and easily.

INSTRUCTIONS

Cut 2 pieces of green fabric 5-1/2" x 20-1/2" and 2 pieces 5-1/2" x 30". With right sides together, pin the 2 shorter pieces to opposite edges of the white fabric. Pin the 2 long pieces to the other opposite edges by centering the strips. Sew green strips to white fabric. Press seams open and topstitch 1/8" inside green strips. Make a 1/4" hem along edges of green strips. Make knots with ends of long strips.

Appliques: Trace the motifs on the applique fabric. Lay applique fabric over fusible web and cut out both thicknesses at once. Make 4 cucumbers, cutting out 4 pieces of the inside and outside motifs. Cut out 2 peppers and 2 stalks of celery. Trace the outside of the cucumber on green cotton fabric and the inside of cucumber, the celery and pepper on light green fabric. Iron on each cucumber applique in each corner with the light green piece on the dark green piece. Iron the other appliques where you desire. With felt-tip pen, draw the seeds.

NAPKINS

FINISHED MEASUREMENTS

18-1/2" x 18-1/2"

MATERIALS

White cotton fabric 16-1/2" x 16-1/2", green-and -white-striped cotton fabric about 6" x 59", sewing machine thread. For the appliques: light green and green cotton, fusible web (see note for bread basket napkin), green felt-tip fabric marker.

INSTRUCTIONS

Make a 1/4" hem along all edges of white fabric. Cut 2 strips green/white striped fabric 2-1/4" x 59". Sew the short ends of the fabric, right sides together. Sew short ends to form a ring. Make a 1/4" hem along one edge. Run 2 rows of basting thread along the other edge of the fabric and gather until total width is 63". Pin the white fabric over the gathered edge of the ruffle, adjusting gathers as you go. Sew in place. Trim the ruffled seam. Cut out appliques from fabric and fusible web, as with the bread basket liner, and press in place. Place a motif in 1 corner of each napkin.

PLACE MATS

FINISHED MEASUREMENTS

13" x 19-3/4"

MATERIALS

1/2 yd of green-and-white-striped fabric 59" wide, green cotton fabric 13-3/4" x 20-1/2", 1-1/4 yd green/white striped seam binding, pencil, iron-on fabric, tracing paper, sewing machine thread.

Note: To make the place mats more durable, you may want to zigzag stitch the border in place.

INSTRUCTIONS

Cut 2 pieces of striped fabric 13-3/4" x 20-1/2". Trace the scallop border motif onto tracing paper, extending the motif to next corner and forming a square. Pin to iron-on fabric and cut out. Place on a piece of striped fabric. Iron on. Place second piece of striped fabric on first, right sides facing. Sew along 3 edges. Turn right side out. Turn in seam allowance on last side and sew in place. Cut seam binding in 2 equal pieces. Fold right sides together and sew along 2 long sides. Turn inside out, turn in ends, and sew in place. Fold the strip in half and center the strip on the wrong side of the place mat about 3" from 1 short end. Tack the center of the strip in place. ∎

Pattern on next page.

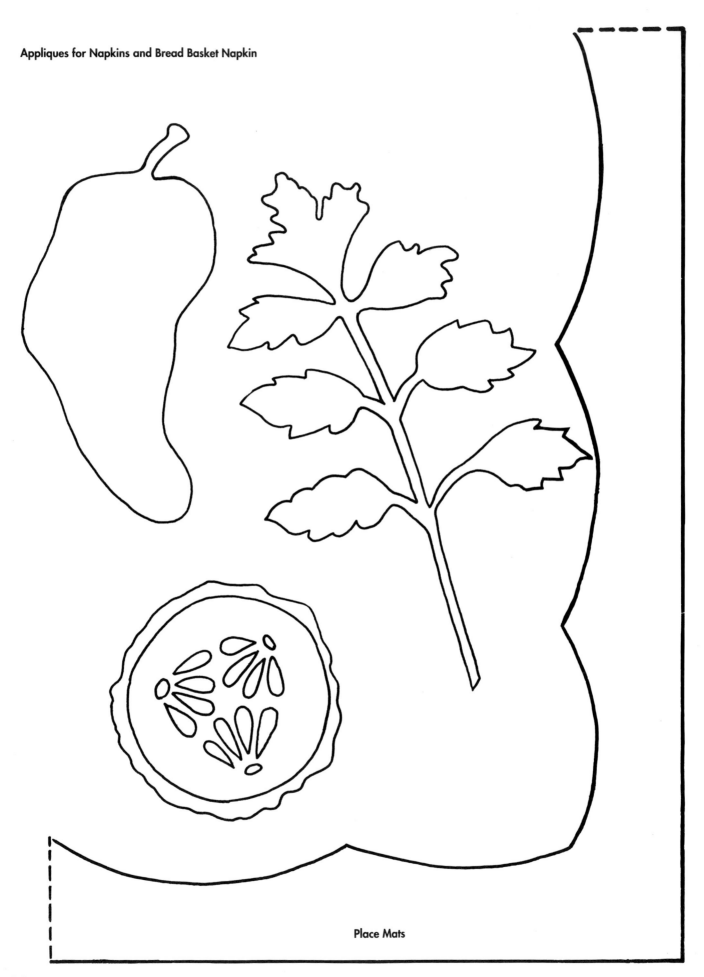

Place Mats

CHRISTMAS PACKAGES

PAGE 76

MATERIALS

6 small boxes or blocks of plastic foam in different shapes and sizes, small pieces of Christmas design fabric or wrapping paper, glue or tape, red thread, 20" of red ribbon 2" wide, thin red ribbon, scissors and corsage pins.

INSTRUCTIONS

Wrap the boxes or foam blocks and tape or glue the wrapping in place. Cut thin ribbon and tie around the packages. Cut different lengths of thin ribbons and attach to the back of each package. Join the ends of all the ribbons and pin to the corner of the table. With wide ribbon, make a double bow and pin over the package ribbons. ■

STIFFY BOWS FOR TABLECLOTH

PAGE 77

FINISHED MEASUREMENTS

Each hanging bow is about 13-3/4" x 17-3/4". Tabletop bow 4" x 17-3/4".

MATERIALS

1 yd of printed fabric 45" wide, white glue, paper towel rolls, clear lacquer, 3 safety pins.

CORNER STIFFY BOWS

INSTRUCTIONS

Cut 3 strips of fabric 8" wide: one 29-1/2" long, and two 31-1/2" long. Cut a square 4" x 4". Mix 1 part white glue with 2 parts water and brush on both sides of the long strips. Fold the long strips long sides together, so that they're 4" wide.

Cut the ends of the shorter strip to form V's as shown in sketch. Fold the square so that it is now 4" x 2" (2 ends meeting at the center). Let the pieces dry until they are just barely damp, about 1 to 1-1/2 hours. Form 2 loops with each of the 2 longer strips: just fold the 2 longer strips so the ends meet at the center. Fold the shorter strips in half and place at center point of longer strips. Wrap the small 4" x 2" piece to hold all the pieces together. Insert toilet paper tubes in the loops to hold their shape until dry. When the bow is completely dry, remove the tubes. Use spray lacquer, available in paint or hobby shops, to set the shape.

Pin a bow in each corner of a rectangular or square table. For round tablecloth, mark 4 equally spaced positions.

TABLETOP BOW

INSTRUCTIONS

Make 2 unequal loops out of each long strip. Lay the short strip flat, place the 2 looped strips joining at center, and fold the short strip over the joined ends. Use the photo as a guide. ■

Instructions continued on next page.

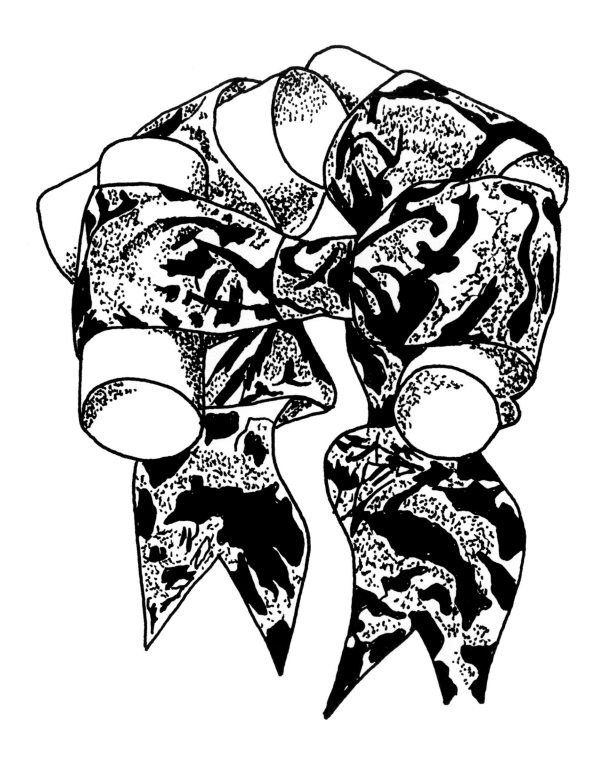

Insert toilet paper tubes in the loops
to hold the bow's shape until dry.

TABLE LINENS WITH RIBBONS

TIPS FOR PULLING RIBBONS THROUGH FABRIC

Any fabric with a linen-like weave and with threads that don't rip too easily is ideal. Important: Leaving an even or uneven number of threads as space between ribbons will create different patterns. It is recommended to practice first with a small piece of fabric before starting with a tablecloth. If by any chance a thread rips or if a wrong thread has been pulled out, use a darning needle and weave it back in again.

PLACE MAT WITH SATIN RIBBONS

FINISHED MEASUREMENTS

12-1/2" x 17"

MATERIALS

20" of white Aida cloth 56" wide. One-sided satin ribbon 1/3" wide: about 50" each of pink, yellow, orange and about 2-1/2 yds of gray. Double sided satin ribbon 1/8" wide: about 5 yds of gray.

INSTRUCTIONS

Cut a 16-1/2" x 20-3/4" piece of fabric and fray the outer 1-1/4". (This will make it easy to pull out the threads. Later the fringe will be trimmed off.) For the 1/4" wide ribbons pull out 3 threads, for the 1/3" wide ribbons pull out 7 threads. Before pulling out the last thread connect the loop of a double sewing thread to it which is then pulled into the fabric at the same time as the original thread is being pulled out. Disconnect the original thread and put the desired satin ribbon into the loop of the sewing thread. Pull the sewing thread out of the fabric and at the same time pull the satin ribbon in.

Start with the two shorter sides of the place mat about 4" from the edge using the following colors: gray (1/8"), skip 2 threads for space between ribbons, pink (1/3"), 2 thread space, gray (1/8"), 2 thread space, yellow (1/3"), 2 thread space, gray (1/8"), 2 thread space, orange (1/3"), 2 thread space, gray (1/8"). Then pull the ribbons through the longer side 8" from the edge using the same color sequence but leaving a space of 3 threads between each ribbon.

Trim the outer 1-1/4" off. Make a double hem 1/3" wide with mitered corners. Sew the 1/3" wide gray satin ribbon around the edges of the place mat.

PATTERN WITH WIDE AND NARROW RIBBONS

MATERIALS

White Aida cloth 56" wide, one-sided satin ribbon 1/3" wide in orange, yellow, pink, cream, double sided satin ribbon 1/8" wide in orange, yellow, pink, cream.

INSTRUCTIONS

Pull 3 threads out of the linen for the 1/8" wide ribbons and 7 threads for the 1/3" wide ribbons. Pull the satin ribbons in following previous instructions, but leaving only a space of 1 thread between the ribbons. Start with the wide ribbons on the longer side. Color sequence: orange, yellow, pink, cream. Then pull in the narrow ribbons on the shorter side working in the same color sequence as before.

PATTERN WITH PEARL COTTON

MATERIALS

White uneven weave fabric, pearl cotton in gray, pink, yellow, beige, orange.

INSTRUCTIONS

This fabric has squares woven in which are created by thread "bundles": the warp consists of 3 threads, the weft of 6 threads. These thread bundles are now replaced by embroidery floss. Pull out most threads of a bundle, leaving just 2 threads in. Tie the embroidery floss to these and pull it through the fabric. Color sequence of the pattern shown: for the weft all threads are gray, for the warp repeat yellow, pink, beige, orange.

PATTERN WITH WIDE SPACES BETWEEN RIBBONS

MATERIALS

White Aida cloth 56" wide, one-sided satin ribbon 1/3" wide in yellow and cream, double-sided satin ribbon 1/8" wide in gray and pink.

INSTRUCTIONS

Pull out 3 threads for the 1/8" wide ribbons and 7 threads for the 1/3" wide ribbons. The space between ribbons is 6 threads. Pull the ribbons through as described previously. Color sequence horizontally: gray (1/8"), cream (1/3"), pink (1/8"), yellow (1/3"), gray (1/8"). Vertically: pink (1/8"), cream (1/3"), gray (1/8"), yellow (1/3") and pink (1/8").

PATTERN WITH NARROW RIBBONS

MATERIALS

White Aida cloth 56" wide, double-sided satin ribbon 1/8" wide in gray, fuchsia, yellow, orange, cream.

INSTRUCTIONS

Pull out 3 threads each for the 1/8" wide ribbons. Work the ribbons into the fabric following the previous instructions. Color and pattern sequence: gray, 3 thread space, fuchsia, 3 thread space, yellow, 6 thread space, then without a space between ribbons: orange, gray, fuchsia and yellow, 6 thread space, fuchsia, 3 thread space, cream, 3 thread space, gray, 6 thread space, orange.

PATTERN ON SYNTHETIC VOILE

MATERIALS

Synthetic voile with linen weave, one sided satin ribbon about 1/4" wide in pink (117), double-sided satin ribbon 1/8" wide in pink, orange, gray and double-sided satin ribbon 1/2" wide in pink and gray.

INSTRUCTIONS

Pull as many threads as needed for the width of each ribbon making sure it is always an uneven number. Pull the satin ribbons into the fabric as described previously. The space between the ribbons on the shown pattern is always 11 threads. Color sequence: pink (1/2"), orange (1/8"), pink (1/3"), gray (1/8"), pink (1/2"), pink (1/3"), pink (1/8") and gray (1/2"). ■

TABLECLOTH WITH RIBBONS

PAGE 80

FINISHED MEASUREMENTS

59" x 74-3/4"

MATERIALS

2-1/4 yds cream white linen 26 threads per inch or rough cotton fabric, 14-3/4 yds of pink ribbon 1/4" wide, 4 yds of blue ribbon 1/4" wide, a large darning needle with a dull point, a sewing needle, basting thread, braided seam binding.

INSTRUCTIONS

Make 1/4" channels through which you will pull ribbons. Pull out horizontal threads for horizontal channels and vertical threads for vertical channels. Place the first channel 3-1/2" from the outside edges. Make a 2nd channel 20" from the first channel. Start outside border 3-1/2" from the outside edges. Thread pink ribbon (held by a large darning needle) under and over 8 threads. Tack ends to wrong side of fabric. For inside ribbons, along the short sides, thread blue ribbon, and along long sides, thread pink ribbon. Work over 26 threads and under 4 threads. Adjust as necessary so pink ribbon overlaps blue ribbon and ribbon is woven under 4 threads at all 4 sides of juncture. (See photo.) Tack ends in place. Make 4 pink bows and tack to corners of tabletop ribbons. Make 4 blue bows and tack to corners of tablecloth. Make a hem 1-1/4" with a 1/4" inner hem and mitered corners. ■

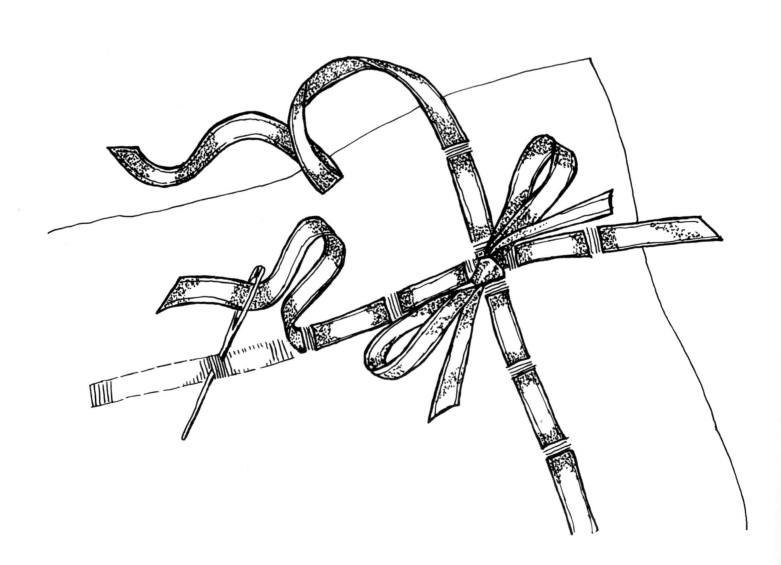

STITCHERY

This circle of flowers and butterflies uses only four kinds of stitches: cross stitch, stem stitch, satin stitch, and French knots. Like most large, circular motifs, it looks best on a round table. (See detail, page 15.)

Instructions for this project are found on page 113.

STITCHERY

V ivid red stitchery shows up beautifully on a crisp white tablecloth. Both the stylized carnations in the center and the lilies in
the corners are worked in cross stitch. A border ties it all together.

INSTRUCTIONS FOR THIS PROJECT
ARE FOUND ON PAGE 115.

STITCHERY

*T*his blue-and-white place mat is a veritable sampler of embroidery stitches, but none is particularly difficult. Most are variations of a few well-known stitches. (See detail, page 2.)

INSTRUCTIONS FOR THIS PROJECT
ARE FOUND ON PAGE 116.

STITCHERY

Cutwork embroidery can be striking, especially when the finished piece is displayed on a contrasting color that shows through the open spaces. To do cutwork embroidery, outline the areas to be cut out in outline stitch, then re-work the outlines in buttonhole stitch. Finally, cut out the outlined areas.

INSTRUCTIONS FOR THIS PROJECT ARE FOUND ON PAGE 118.

STITCHERY

*T*hese handsome place mats
add another flourish to cutwork embroidery: bars across
the open spaces. The bars are
simply three strands of thread
worked from outline to outline
before the areas are cut.

INSTRUCTIONS FOR THIS PROJECT
ARE FOUND ON PAGE 120.

STITCHERY

*B*elow: *These charming folkloric motifs are worked in cross stitch. For a more traditional look, they can be worked on white fabric rather than red. Right: Herbs are perfect motifs for table linen. The sprig of sage and the pepper plant will add zest to a light lunch or a full-course meal.*

INSTRUCTIONS FOR THESE PROJECTS
ARE FOUND ON PAGES 121 AND 122.

STITCHERY

Below: *One advantage of embroidering with huge stitches is that they look dramatic. Another is that the work takes half the time. These enormous roses will enliven the most subdued dinner party.*
Right: This elegant white-on-white cloth is embroidered in pearl cotton, with fans alternately outlined in stem stitch and filled in with cross stitch.

INSTRUCTIONS FOR THESE PROJECTS ARE FOUND ON PAGES 123 AND 125.

STITCHERY

I n spite of the heavy embroidery, this tablecloth is an easy one to make. There's only one stitch—a simple running stitch—worked in various lengths. The rows of stitches change from light blue to yellow to red to pink and so on down the cloth.

INSTRUCTIONS FOR THIS PROJECT ARE FOUND ON PAGE 126.

STITCHERY

T*he apples and pears on this place mat will linger long after the tart is eaten and the dishes washed. Vivid in red and yellow, this mat would make a perfect gift.*

INSTRUCTIONS FOR THIS PROJECT
ARE FOUND ON PAGE 127.

STITCHERY

T he fir trees on this pale green linen cloth suggest a quiet Christmas spirit. Patterns for trees in five different sizes are given with the instructions. Overlap them any way you like, and work them in large cross stitches, for a rustic, casual look. A row of cross stitches provides a border and gives the trees something to stand on. Work each matching napkin with a tree of its own.

INSTRUCTIONS FOR THIS PROJECT
ARE FOUND ON PAGE 128.

STITCHERY

W̲orked in purple and green cotton thread, these cross stitch stars look rich and dark against a pale gray tablecloth. An embroidered border gives the cloth a finished look.

INSTRUCTIONS FOR THIS PROJECT
ARE FOUND ON PAGE 129.

STITCHERY

*C*hristmas roses, winter heather, and fallen leaves form a beautiful wreath on this tablecloth of ecru linen. Forty shades of embroidery floss appear in the pattern, for a wonderful variety of colors. The pattern works best on a round tablecloth.

INSTRUCTIONS FOR THIS PROJECT
ARE FOUND ON PAGE 130.

STITCHERY

A table's not just for eating on. It's also for playing on. At your next card party, this marvelous cloth will distract your opponents and give you the upper hand. Patterns for all four card suits are included with the directions.

INSTRUCTIONS FOR THIS PROJECT
ARE FOUND ON PAGE 132.

Stitchery

Wild flowers embroidered on light green linen have a country look. A few butterflies have fluttered by and stayed for dinner. Chain stitch is the dominant technique for this project, but other stitches appear as well: satin and daisy stitches, stem stitch and back stitch, and, as ever when there are flowers with centers, French knots.

INSTRUCTIONS FOR THIS PROJECT ARE FOUND ON PAGE 134.

A fruit wreath is an appetizing centerpiece. This playful ring is worked in chain stitch, stem stitch, satin stitch, and French knots, in bright, cheerful colors. Matching napkins can be worked using any of the individual fruits that strike your fancy.

INSTRUCTIONS FOR THIS PROJECT
ARE FOUND ON PAGE 136.

STITCHERY

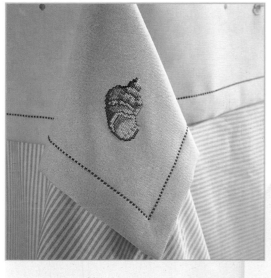

O pposite page: Decorated napkins can be just as memorable as an embroidered tablecloth. If you know what you're going to serve, you can select your motif to match your menu. Below: Seashells and starfish are worked in cross stitch on this pale pink cloth, with a confetti of satin stitches scattered about. The result is a lighthearted table setting, ready for a delicate shrimp salad or a hearty bouillabaisse.

INSTRUCTIONS FOR THESE PROJECTS ARE FOUND ON PAGES 138 AND 140.

STITCHERY

Pansies are among the most cheerful flowers. Worked in cross stitch with a satin stitch border and stem stitch stems, these big, cheerful blooms will brighten even the grayest afternoon.

INSTRUCTIONS FOR THIS PROJECT
ARE LOCATED ON PAGE 141.

Tablecloth with Blue Butterflies

PAGE 91

FINISHED MEASUREMENTS

20-1/2" diameter tabletop, cloth 54-1/4" diameter

MATERIALS

55" x 55" pearl gray even-weave cotton with 28 threads per inch, DMC floss in indicated colors, 178" bias binding in desired colors.

INSTRUCTIONS

Mark the center horizontal and vertical centers of cloth with basting thread. Embroider the motifs in cross stitch using 2 strands of floss over 2 threads of cloth. Where 2 colors are given in the Key to Chart, use 1 strand of each color. Begin motif at point A, 280 threads from the center. Repeat the motif 4 times total. Embroider in stem stitch using 2 strands of floss: color mustard #739 on the flowers, color dark blue #824 around the full butterflies and medium blue #517 around the closed butterflies. Embroider the stamens of the flowers in satin stitch in mustard #739 and french knots in 1 strand of color dark brown #839.

Cut out cloth to a diameter of 54-1/4". Unfold bias binding and sew 1/2 to right side of tablecloth edges, fold to wrong side and hem in place. ■

KEY TO CHART FOR TABLECLOTH WITH FLOWERS AND BUTTERFLIES

		DMC
⊞	= light green	472
L	= light green	3348
⊙	= light green	704
⊠	= light green	703
◎	= light green	702
▼	= dark green	905
⋮	= white	white
◪	= dark brown	839
⊠	= brown	420
⊡	= light blue	747
⊡	= light blue	519
⊿	= light blue	518/519
◩	= light blue	518
⊠	= light blue	517
■	= dark blue	824

Pattern continued on next page.

Pattern continued from previous page.

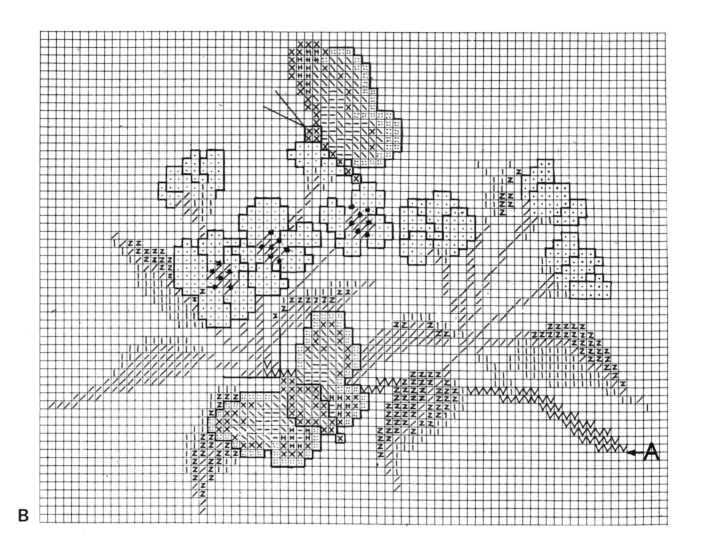

B

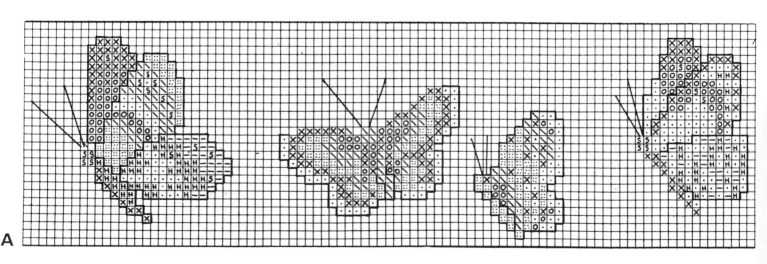

A

TABLECLOTH WITH RED CARNATIONS

PAGE 92

FINISHED MEASUREMENTS

56" x 56"

Measurements of the embroidery:
15-3/4" x 15-3/4"

MATERIALS

White fabric 56" wide with about
30 threads to the inch, 7 skeins of
embroidery floss in cherry red

INSTRUCTIONS

Secure the edges of the tablecloth with
zigzag stitch to prevent fraying. Mark
the horizontal and vertical center of
the tablecloth with basting stitch.
Work the center motif from the

marked center following the chart.
Work the corner motif D four times at
an equal distance of 8" from the center
(100 cross stitches or 200 threads).
Add 4 additional small motifs to each
side of the corner motif. Turn the
tablecloth by 90° when embroidering
each corner motif.

Press the embroidery on the wrong
side. Make a 1/2" hem with a 1/4"
inner hem and mitered corners. ■

KEY TO CHART FOR TABLECLOTH
WITH RED EMBROIDERY

o = cherry red

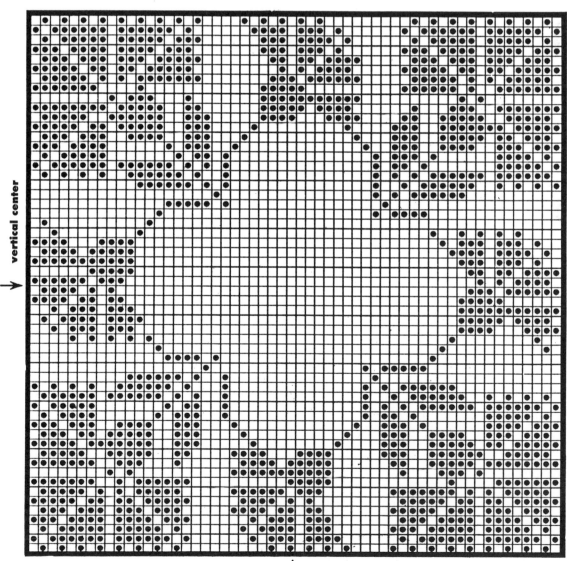

vertical center

horizontal center

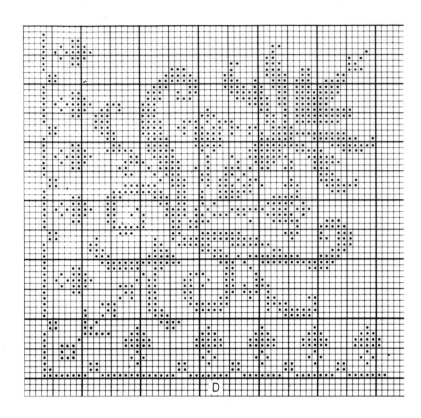

der, 2-1/2" from the side and lower edge. Use the following stitches: satin, square, star, v-, holbein, cross, double-cross stitch, herringbone, stem, outline, and running stitch.

Cut the fabric 1-3/4" from the outside of the border. Make a 1/2" hem with mitered corners. ■

BLUE AND WHITE PLACE MATS

PAGE 93

FINISHED MEASUREMENTS

16-1/4" x 20-1/2"

MATERIALS

3/4 yd white even-weave fabric 56" wide with 19 threads per inch, pearl cotton (single strand embroidery cotton) in light blue and blue

INSTRUCTIONS

Cut fabric to 21-3/4" x 25-1/2". Embroider using 1 strand of pearl cotton, following the chart. Each square equals 1 strand. Embroider the thick lines in blue and light lines in light blue. Begin at the right side of the bor-

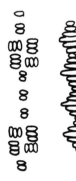

V-Stitch

Zigzag

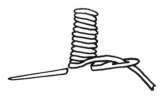

Satin Stitch

116

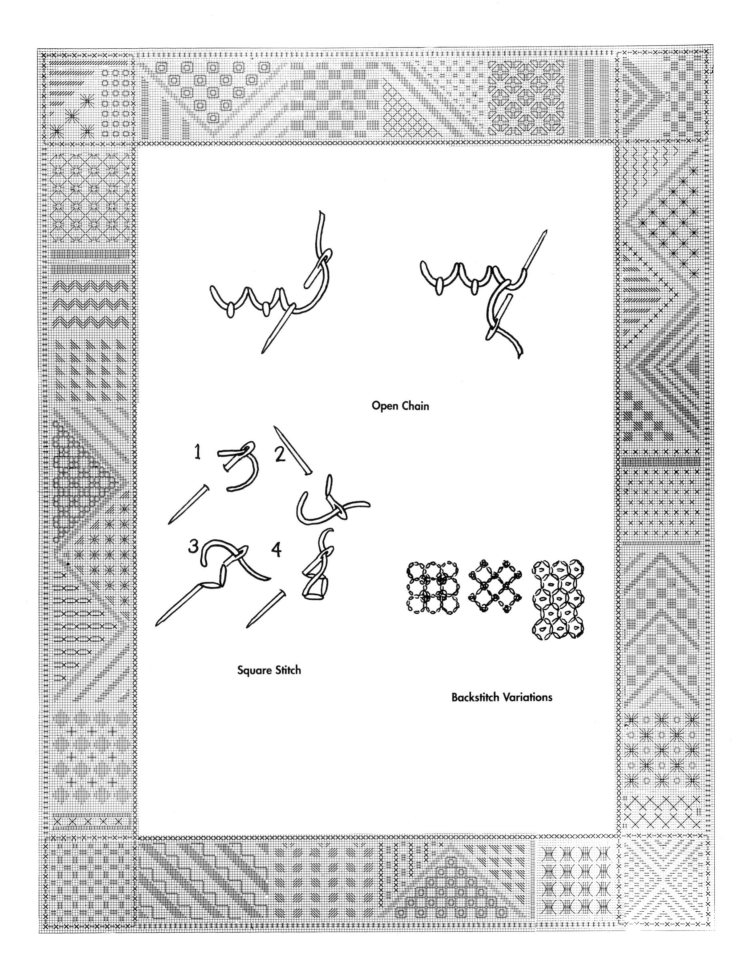

Open Chain

1   2

3   4

Square Stitch

Backstitch Variations

TIPS FOR CUTWORK EMBROIDERY

Outline the motif in outline stitch. Work thin lines first, embroidering over the exact same threads with each stitch as shown in the drawing. Keep the stitches very close together.

Work over the outline stitches with blanket stitch. The ends of the previously embroidered lines should be covered over in the outline.

With sharp scissors, cut out the fabric as indicated. Be very careful not to cut any of the stitches. ■

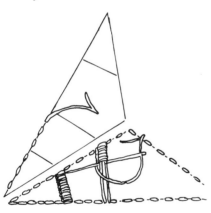

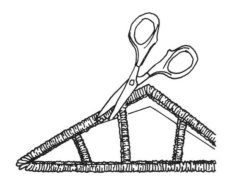

TABLECLOTH WITH CUTWORK GRAPES

PAGE 94

FINISHED MEASUREMENTS

53-1/4" x 53-1/4"

MATERIALS

1-1/2 yds of white linen fabric 55" wide, DMC embroidery cotton in pink #754 and DMC embroidery floss.

Note: Trace the motif on a piece of paper, then pin to the pressed fabric. (Black sections indicate areas which will be cut out.) With a strand of embroidery floss, make a running stitch outline around all the motifs. Then work in buttonhole or blanket stitch around the outlines. Make each stitch about 1/16" to 1/8" long. For thin lines between openwork sections, be sure to work carefully over the same number of threads. With very sharp scissors, cut out the openwork sections.

INSTRUCTIONS

Place the tracing paper over the corner of the tablecloth about 3/4" from the edge of one corner. The veins of the leaves and the tendril on the right are worked using 3 strands of floss. The broad stems of the bunch are worked in padded satin stitch (first fill in area with chain stitch). The top of the stem is outlined in blanket stitch using embroidery cotton. Embroider the small stems using 2 strands of embroidery floss. All blanket stitch outlines are worked in embroidery cotton. Work the edges of the tablecloth in blanket stitch. With sharp scissors cut out the openwork sections and around curves of outline at corner. ■

CUTWORK
PLACE MATS

PAGE 95

FINISHED MEASUREMENTS

17-1/4" x 13-1/4"

Measurements of embroidery:
about 2-1/2" x 12-1/4"

MATERIALS

18" of white embroidery linen 60" wide. Anchor embroidery floss #16: For both place mats, 2 skeins of white #2 and 1 skein each of peach #48, powder pink #50, light sea green #185 and mint green #203.

INSTRUCTIONS

For one place mat cut a 21-1/4" x 17-1/4" piece of fabric and secure with zigzag stitch to prevent fraying. Mark the center line between the two shorter sides with basting stitch. Copy the pattern onto tracing paper, then draw it mirror image to the paper's center line. Transfer the whole pattern with dressmaker's carbon 3-1/2" from the upper edge onto the fabric so that the center lines of the pattern and the fabric match.

Embroider the double lines of the motif first with small outline stitches in the correct color. Work the bars at the same time by working the thread 3 times across the fabric from outline to outline. Then embroider over the threads with buttonhole stitch (see the chart). Finally work over all the double lines with buttonhole stitch. Be careful to do the parts of the motif that seem to be lower first and then embroider the prominent parts. The loops of the buttonhole stitches should point toward the area that will be cut out later.

Distribution of colors: Work the lower three flower petals of the bottom place mat and the arc over the flower of the top place mat in peach, the remaining flower petals in powder pink (see photo). Work the four upper leaves in both place mats in mint green and the two lower leaves in light sea green.

Press the embroidery on the wrong side. Then cut out the fabric along the buttonhole stitches (gray area on the chart) using very sharp pointed scissors. Make a double hem 1" wide with mitered corners. ∎

(Half the pattern)

Shown 78% of actual size.
Photocopy at 128%.

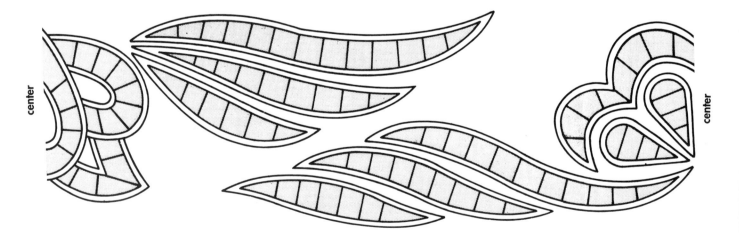

center

center

Double lines mark the border of the motif; single lines mark the bars.

Tablecloth with Folkloric Motifs

PAGE 96

FINISHED MEASUREMENTS

67" x 48-1/4", with a 6-1/2" wide motif

MATERIALS

2 yds of red or white cotton fabric about 55" wide with 18 threads per inch, DMC Cotton Lustre #980 in indicated colors (1 ball for each color) or DMC embroidery floss.

Note: If using embroidery floss, use 4 strands for embroidery.

INSTRUCTIONS

Embroider the motifs in cross stitch, following the chart and working each stitch over 2 threads. Place lower edge of chart 4" from lower edge of cloth. Begin with a corner motif and one long side of work. Repeat the motif 4 times along each long side between corner motifs. Repeat the motif 3 times along each narrow side between corner motifs.

Fold 1-1/2" along edge to inside and press, making mitered corners. Fold 1-1/2" to inside and press for a 1-1/2" hem. Hemstitch in place. ■

KEY TO CHART FOR TABLECLOTH

	DMC Cotton Lustre	Embroidery Floss
⧅ = Pink	8771	604
□ = Orange	8727	740
⊡ = Light Blue	8756	996
◙ = Blue	8709	797
⊠ = Green	8736	702

Repeat

Corner Motif

HERB
PLACE MATS

PAGE 97

FINISHED MEASUREMENTS

13-3/4" x 18-3/4"

MATERIALS

1/2 yd of white even-weave cloth
(such as hardanger) 56" wide, 26
threads per inch. 1 skein of Anchor
embroidery floss for each color, using
4 strands of floss for the cross stitch
and 3 strands of floss for the backstitch.

Place mat with peppers: olive green
#266, brick red #13, salmon #10 and
orange #925.

Place mat with sage: olive green #266,
dark green #246, dark red #59, light
salmon #9 and light pink-red #76.

INSTRUCTIONS

Cut 17-3/4" x 21-1/2" of fabric and
secure the edges with zigzag stitch, to
prevent fraying. Start the embroidery
with the border 2-1/4" from all edges
beginning in one corner. The border
has 109 cross stitches on the short
sides and 147 cross stitches on the
long sides. Work each cross stitch
over 3 threads.

Press the embroidery on the wrong
side and trim the material leaving 1-
1/2" from the embroidered border.
Make a 1/2" hem with a 1/4" inner
hem and mitered corners. ■

KEY TO CHART FOR PLACE MATS
WITH HERB MOTIFS

⊠ = orange   #925
⊡ = light salmon   #9
⊠ = salmon   #10
⊿ = light pink-red #76
⊞ = brick red   #13
⊟ = dark red   #59
···or●= olive green #266
   for back stitch)
─ or ◢ = dark green #246
   (also for back stitch)

Pepper

Sage

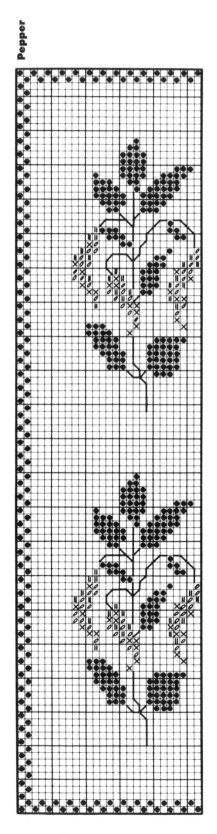

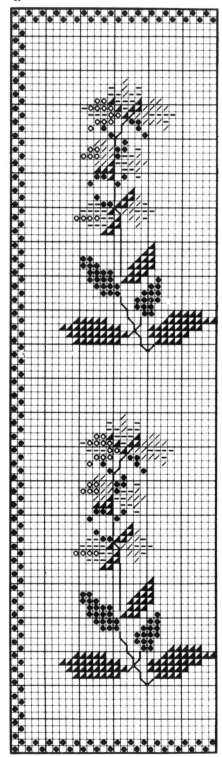

122

Rose
Tablecloth

PAGE 98

FINISHED MEASUREMENTS

54-1/2" x 73-3/4". Border width 8-1/2". Oval 29" x 17-1/4".

MATERIALS

2-1/4 yds white linen about 67" wide with 35 threads per inch, DMC embroidery floss.

INSTRUCTIONS

Mark the horizontal and vertical center of the tablecloth. Embroider the motifs in cross stitch, following the charts. Use 2 strands of floss and work over 5 threads for each cross stitch on the center oval. Use 3 strands of floss and work over 7 threads for each cross stitch on the border. Center the oval at point M on one long side 300 threads down from the center. Work the second half of the motif to correspond. Center the edge motif at point A, 878 threads from the center (578 threads from the oval motif). Work the second half to correspond.

Cut the cloth to 60" x 79-1/3". Fold the edges 1-1/2" from the lowest edge of embroidery and press in place, folding top of hem to inside. Make mitered corners. ■

**Pattern continued
on next page.**

DMC

◣ = Dark blue   820
◩ = Blue   798
◨ = Orange   608
⊡ = Pink   962
◉ = Dark pink   3350
⊠ = Dark purple   552
◰ = Lilac   554
☐ = Light lilac   211
⊠ = Green   987
◺ = Light green   368

Pattern continued from previous page.

WHITE ON WHITE TABLECLOTH

PAGE 99

FINISHED MEASUREMENTS

51-1/4" x 67"

MATERIALS

2-1/4" white linen 63" wide with 28 threads per inch, DMC or Anchor gray pearl cotton color #762 or #397.

INSTRUCTIONS

With basting thread, mark the horizontal and vertical center of the fabric. Embroider the square center motif in cross stitch, following the chart. Make each cross stitch using 1 strand pearl cotton over 3 threads. Begin the embroidery on one long side 12" from the center at point M. Embroider the motif 5 times to the corner. Embroider the corner motif, then work repeat 6 times total, work corner motif, work repeat 10 times to corner, complete motif. (There will be 21 motifs along the long sides and 13 along the short sides.) The center motif is 24-1/2" x 59".

In the left corner, embroider 1 corner motif in cross stitch following the chart in cross stitch. Begin 78 threads under the corner of the center motif. Embroider 1 fan in other 3 corners, reverse motif to correspond to corner. 11" from the corner of the center motif, embroider 1 corner fan motif, then work 7 fan motifs along each long side (centering one at center marker) and 5 fan motifs along each narrow side. Work fans next to corner motif in stem stitch and alternate fans in cross stitch. Use 1 strand pearl cotton over 3 threads for each cross stitch. Remove basting thread.

Trim the edges to 5-1/2" below fan motifs. Two threads above the hem, make an openwork hem 1-1/2" wide with mitered corners. Gather 3 threads in each stitch, using 1 strand of pearl cotton and working above the hem only. (Do not gather threads at upper edge of openwork hem.) ■

Corner Motif

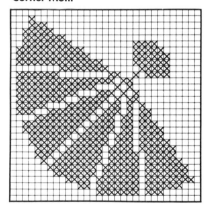

Fan Motif

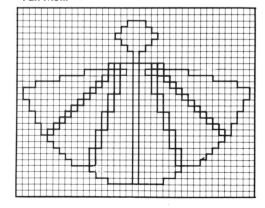

Border Chart

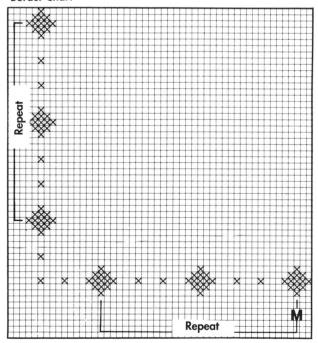

TABLECLOTH WITH RUNNING STITCH

PAGE 100

FINISHED MEASUREMENTS

51-1/2" x 66-1/2". Hem width: 3-1/4"

MATERIALS

2 yds black cotton fabric 55" wide
with 25 threads per inch, DMC
embroidery cotton #16.

Note: The embroidery is worked by
following the chart.

INSTRUCTIONS

Begin chart at point A at one corner,
3-1/4" from the edge. Each square
equals 2 threads on the tablecloth.
Work 1 long side first. After the corner motif, there will be a half motif,
29 full motifs and a half motif, then
the corner motif. The short side will
have a half motif, 21 full motifs, a half
motif, then the corner motif. Continue
around.

Measure 1-1/2" below the lower edge
of embroidery and make a hem 1-1/4"
wide, folding in 1/4" to inside of hem
with mitered corners. Hemstitch in
place. ■

EMBROIDERY COLORS FOR
THE TABLECLOTH

	DMC
red	666
pink	604
blue	798
light blue	813
green	703
yellow	743

Apple/Pear Place Mat

PAGE 101

FINISHED MEASUREMENTS

15-3/4" x 15-3/4"

MATERIALS

20" x 20" of beige Aida cloth with 11 double threads per inch. DMC embroidery floss in indicated colors.

INSTRUCTIONS

Embroider the motif in cross stitch, following the chart. Work each stitch using 3 strands of floss worked over 2 double threads. Embroider a square 15" x 15" in cross stitch in red. In each corner, embroider the corner motif and in between work small motifs in cross stitch. For the stem stitch embroidery use 2 strands of floss. Embroider inner square in red cross stitch, extending the chart from one corner motif to the other.

Cut the fabric allowing 1-1/4" outside the red border. Make 1/4" hem with mitered corners. ■

KEY TO CHART

		DMC
⊡ = pale yellow	745
⊟ = light yellow	743
⊠ = yellow	742
⊻ = light brown	436
☯ = brown	434
⊙ = orange	977
⊠ = rust	921
⊡ = red	817
⊘ = light green	471
⊡ = green	367
■ = dark green	935

Stem stitch: dark brown in 838

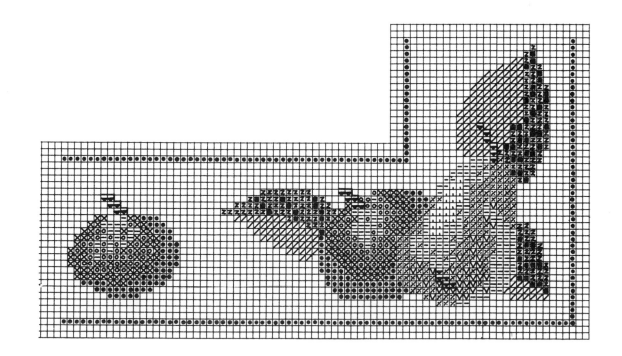

TABLECLOTH AND NAPKINS WITH FIR TREES

PAGE 102

TABLECLOTH

FINISHED MEASUREMENTS

50" x 67"

MATERIALS

2 yds light green linen fabric about 55" wide with 19 threads per inch, DMC embroidery floss in green #912.

Note: The different size tree motifs are given in the pattern. Overlap them as you like to get the desired effect.

INSTRUCTIONS

Make a hem 1-1/4" all around the cloth with mitered corners. At the top of the hem, make a row of green cross stitches using 2 strands of floss, each stitch over 2 threads. Leave 2 threads between each cross stitch. Above the border, work motif of fir trees, overlapping all 5 size trees (see photo).

NAPKINS

FINISHED MEASUREMENTS

5-3/4" x 15-3/4"

MATERIALS

Each napkin: 18" x 18" light green linen with 19 threads per inch, DMC embroidery floss in green #912.

INSTRUCTIONS

Mark the center 15" x 15". Work 1 row of cross stitches around border, using 2 strands of floss, each stitch worked over 2 threads. Leave 2 threads between each cross stitch. Make a hem 1/4" wide with mitered corners. Embroider 1 tree in 1 corner by following the chart beginning 3-1/4" from 1 side and 1-3/4" from lower edge. ■

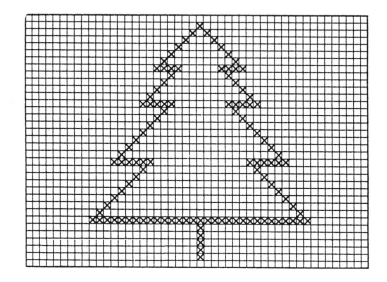

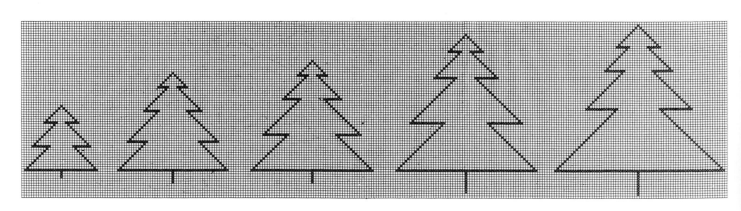

TABLECLOTH WITH PURPLE AND GREEN STARS

PAGE 103

TABLECLOTH

FINISHED MEASUREMENTS

49-1/4" x 49-1/4"

MATERIALS

55" light gray even-weave cloth with 25 threads per inch, embroidery cotton thread in purple and green.

INSTRUCTIONS

Mark the center vertical and horizontal threads. Embroider in cross stitch by following the chart. Work each stitch over 2 threads using 1 strand cotton thread. Begin the chart at point M, 321 threads from the center of the cloth. Work 4 star motifs to the corner, alternately in purple and green, work the corner star in green, make 9 stars to corner. Embroider corner in green and continue around. 4-1/4" from lower edge, embroider small motifs, making sure corner motif is exactly diagonal to the corner motif at center of tablecloth.

Cut the cloth to finished measurements of 54" x 54". Make an inner hem 1/4" wide, then hem the edges, using mitered corners, with the top of the hem below the embroidered border.

NAPKINS

FINISHED MEASUREMENTS

14-3/4" x 14-3/4"

MATERIALS

Light gray even-weave cloth about 17-1/4" x 17-1/4" for each napkin, embroidery cotton thread in green and purple.

INSTRUCTIONS

Embroider a border about 13-3/4" x 13-3/4" centered on the cloth. Work each stitch over 2 threads using 1 strand of cotton thread. Begin at 1 corner 1-3/4" from each edge. Make sure the corners are exactly diagonal from each other.

Make an inner hem 1/2" wide, then hem the edges with the top of the hem below the embroidered border. Miter the corners. ■

KEY TO CHART

⊠ = Green
ⓥ = Purple

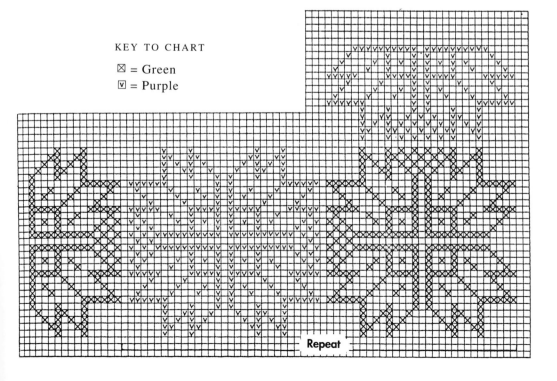

Repeat

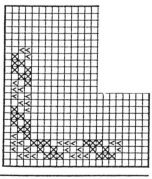

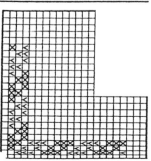

Tablecloth with Roses and Winter Heather

PAGES 104-105

FINISHED MEASUREMENTS

49-1/4" x 49-1/4"

MATERIALS

1-1/2 yds of ecru linen fabric about 55" wide with 28 threads per inch, DMC embroidery floss in indicated colors.

INSTRUCTIONS

Mark the vertical and horizontal center of the cloth with basting thread. Embroider the motifs in cross stitch by following the chart. Use 2 strands of floss over 2 threads. Work stem stitch using 1 strand of floss. Embroider the dots on the heather using color dark brown #610 using 2 strands of floss. Begin embroidery at point A, 300 threads from the beginning. Turn chart 3 times to complete circle.

Make a hem 1-1/4" wide with mitered corners. Work openwork hem, if desired, gathering 3 threads in each stitch. ■

KEY TO CHART FOR TABLECLOTH

	DMC
☑ = bright green	701
⊞ = green	988
● = dark moss green	937
⁚ = bright yellow green	471
◻ = light yellow green	472
◼ = dark green	3345
▨ = medium green	3347
⊟ = light green	3348
% = gray green	320
◹ = light gray green	368
◻ = olive green	734
◻ = light moss green	3013
⊞ = light loden green	3052
⊠ = blue green	501
3 = light teal	502
◠ = pale teal	503
◼ = slate blue	930
⁚ = light gray blue	927
z = gray blue	926
T = khaki	3023
◻ = light gray	3072
◻ = pale taupe	842
■ = brown	610
◻ = rust	356
⊠ = melon	922
o = salmon	402
◼ = medium brown	434
S = honey brown	435
II = golden brown	436
◻ = pale brown	437
◻ = mustard	680
4 = bright yellow	725
L = blond	676
◻ = light blond	677
I = pale yellow	3078
· = white	white
◻ = mauve	3687
N = bright pink	603
≡ = light pink	776
⁚ = dusty rose	778

Stem stitch: Use the same color as the color of the motif, but 1 shade darker or lighter (see photo).

Card-Playing
Tablecloth

PAGES 106-107

FINISHED MEASUREMENTS

51-1/4" x 67"

MATERIALS

2 yds green hardanger cloth 56" wide with 28 threads to the inch, DMC embroidery floss in white, red #666, green #913, gray #414, black #310.

INSTRUCTIONS

Mark the horizontal and vertical center of the cloth. Embroider the cards following the chart. Use 2 strands of floss for each stitch working over 2 threads. Begin the embroidery with the green squares so that the squares are about 13-3/4" x 21-3/4". Begin the squares 1" from the center and space them 2" apart. Embroider the corner motifs, one placed 1" from the outside corner of each square. 1" from the center corner of all the squares, embroider the card motifs.

Make a 1" hem with mitered corners. ■

KEY TO CHART FOR
CORNER MOTIFS

		DMC
⊠ =	red	666
⊡ =	black	310
⊙ =	green	913

KEY TO CHART FOR CARD MOTIFS

		DMC
⊡ =	white	white
⊠ =	red	666
⊻ =	gray	414
⊡ =	black	310

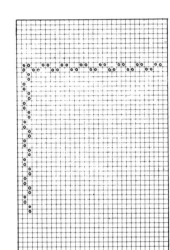

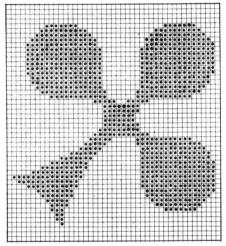

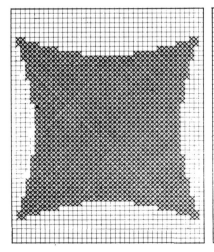

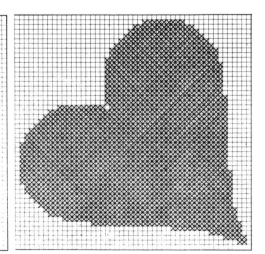

Tablecloth with Flowers and Butterflies

PAGE 108

FINISHED MEASUREMENTS

70-3/4" x 55-1/4". Embroidery 18-3/4" x 44".

MATERIALS

2-1/4 yds light green, tightly woven linen 60" wide, embroidery floss in indicated colors

Note: Work embroidery by following chart.

INSTRUCTIONS

With a basting thread or washable fabric marker, mark the horizontal and vertical center of the cloth. Transfer the design to the cloth. Place the complete flower motifs on the long sides of the cloth, and the center section marked by the dotted line on the narrow sides of cloth. Place point A 8-1/2" down from the center point and point B 21-1/4" from center point.

Embroider the 3 butterfly motifs in 2 opposite corners as you desire, using 3 strands of floss in chain stitch. Embroider the outlines of the white flower petals and the roots in stem stitch, the outlines of the yellow petals in stem or chain stitch, the centers of

the white petals in French knots. Embroider the center of the flowers in satin or chain stitch, and make large daisy stitches for the petals of the large white flower on the left. Fill in the petals with white chain stitches. Embroider the butterflies in chain stitch, outlining in stem stitch. Embroider the antennae in outline stitch.

Fold 3/4" along all edges to inside and press. Make a 1" hem with a 1/4" inner hem and mitered corners. If desired, make an openwork border, gathering about 5 threads in each stitch and wrapping hemming stitches around fabric threads as well. ■

KEY TO CHART FOR TABLECLOTH
WITH FLOWERS AND BUTTERFLIES

		DMC
1 = Blue		792
2 = Green blue		518
3 = Yellow		444
4 = Light yellow		445
5 = Dark green		319
6 = Moss green		469
7 = Light yellow green		471
8 = Gray green		502
9 = Brown		3045
10 = Purple rose		3687
11 = Light pink		3689
12 = Purple		327
13 = White		White
14 = Hunter green		992
15 = Blue green		597
16 = Ecru		712
17 = Gray		645
18 = Old rose		316
19 = Green		3345

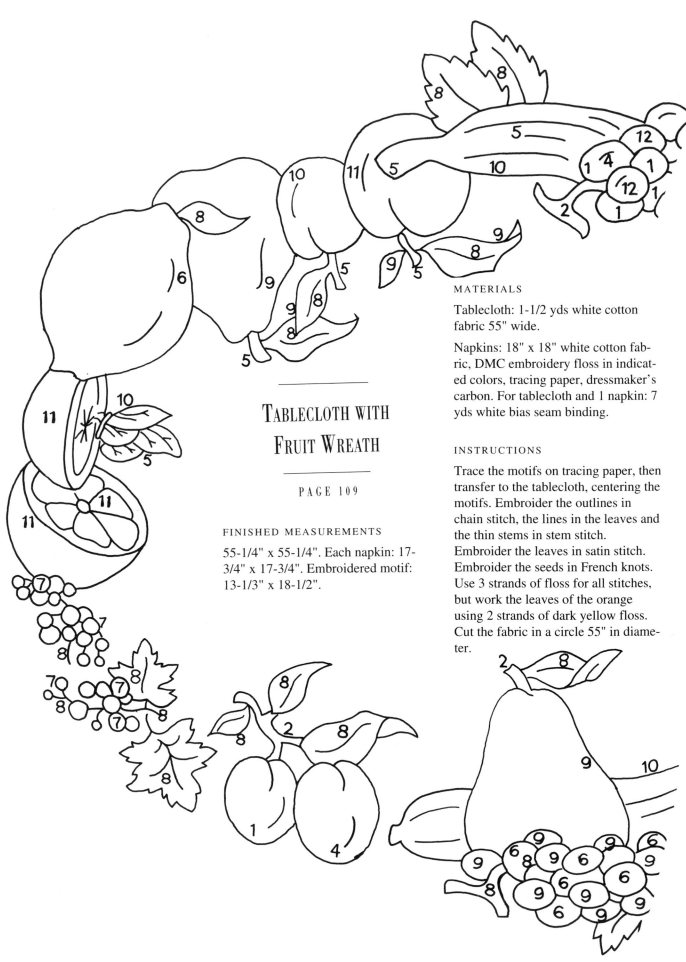

TABLECLOTH WITH FRUIT WREATH

PAGE 109

FINISHED MEASUREMENTS

55-1/4" x 55-1/4". Each napkin: 17-3/4" x 17-3/4". Embroidered motif: 13-1/3" x 18-1/2".

MATERIALS

Tablecloth: 1-1/2 yds white cotton fabric 55" wide.

Napkins: 18" x 18" white cotton fabric, DMC embroidery floss in indicated colors, tracing paper, dressmaker's carbon. For tablecloth and 1 napkin: 7 yds white bias seam binding.

INSTRUCTIONS

Trace the motifs on tracing paper, then transfer to the tablecloth, centering the motifs. Embroider the outlines in chain stitch, the lines in the leaves and the thin stems in stem stitch. Embroider the leaves in satin stitch. Embroider the seeds in French knots. Use 3 strands of floss for all stitches, but work the leaves of the orange using 2 strands of dark yellow floss. Cut the fabric in a circle 55" in diameter.

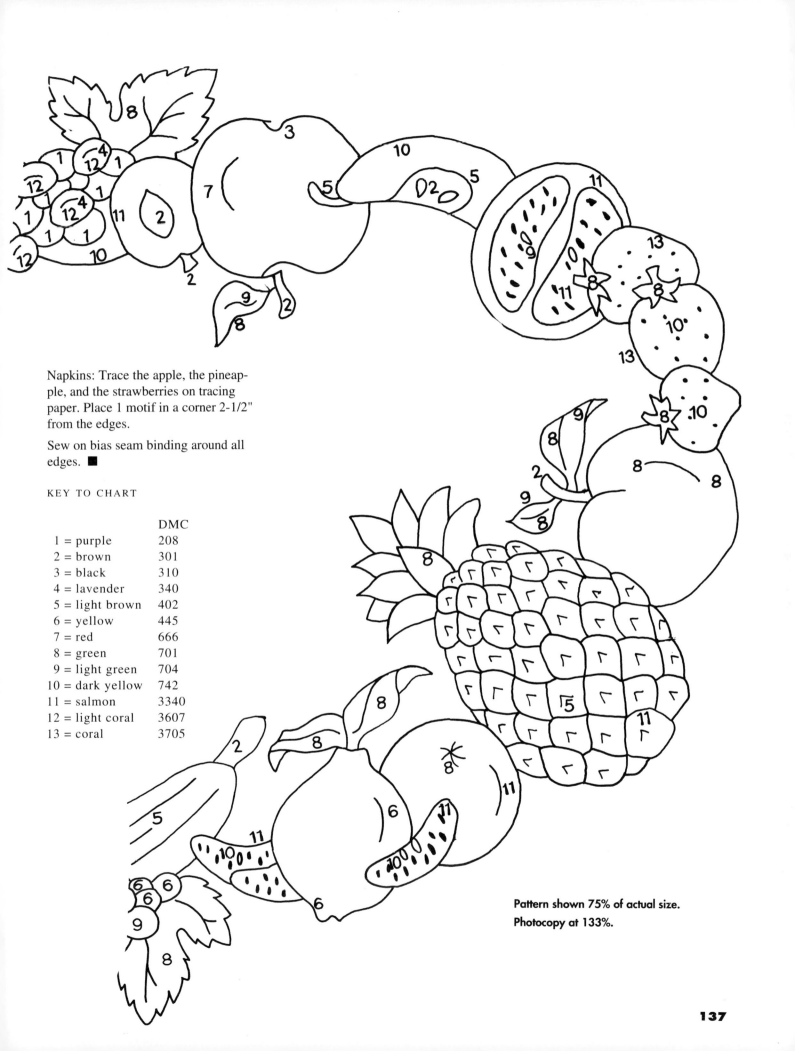

Napkins: Trace the apple, the pineapple, and the strawberries on tracing paper. Place 1 motif in a corner 2-1/2" from the edges.

Sew on bias seam binding around all edges. ■

KEY TO CHART

		DMC
1 =	purple	208
2 =	brown	301
3 =	black	310
4 =	lavender	340
5 =	light brown	402
6 =	yellow	445
7 =	red	666
8 =	green	701
9 =	light green	704
10 =	dark yellow	742
11 =	salmon	3340
12 =	light coral	3607
13 =	coral	3705

Pattern shown 75% of actual size.
Photocopy at 133%.

THREE NAPKINS

PAGE 110

FINISHED MEASUREMENTS

21-3/4" x 21-3/4"

MATERIALS

Aida cloth 11 threads per inch or hardanger cloth with 22 double threads per inch 25-1/2" x 25-1/2", DMC or Anchor embroidery floss in indicated colors, sewing thread.

INSTRUCTIONS

Mark the vertical and horizontal center and the outline of a square 21-3/4" x 21-3/4" with basting thread. Embroider the motif in cross stitch following the chart. Place the motif in the right corner 2" from the basting thread. On hardanger cloth, make each stitch over 2 double threads using 2 strands of floss. On Aida cloth, use 3 strands of floss over each square. Use 1 strand of floss for stem stitch outlines. Make a border 1/4" from basting thread. On the napkin with shell motif, work 3 running stitches next to each other using blue embroidery floss. On the flowered napkin, make a border of square stitches (see sketch) with pink floss. Embroider the fruit napkin in cross stitch in red floss. On hardanger cloth use 2 strands of floss and on Aida cloth use 3 strands of floss. Work each stitch over 2 double threads on hardanger cloth and over 1 block on Aida cloth (on cross stitch border instead of 2 double threads, work over 1 block). Trim fabric to 3/4" from border. Make a hem 1/4" wide with an inner hem and mitered corners. Sew the hem in place. ■

KEY TO CHART FOR
FLOWER MOTIF

		Anchor	DMC
⊙	= dark pink	41	335
▯	= light pink	48	818
⬙	= bright pink	50	605
⬁	= pink	52	956
⬂	= strawberry	54	892
⊡	= lavender	97	554
⊟	= light purple	108	211
⬗	= green	204	913
⊞	= light green	206	955
⊠	= medium green	226	702
⬕	= dark green	230	700
⊞	= yellow green	265	3348
⬔	= moss green	280	472
⬚	= yellow	297	726
⬗	= pale mauve	869	3042
▥	= mauve	870	3041

Stem stitch: outline the purple flowers in dark purple 99 or 553, outline the pink flower in red 46 or 666, outline the light pink flower in old rose 77 or 3687, outline everything else in dark green.

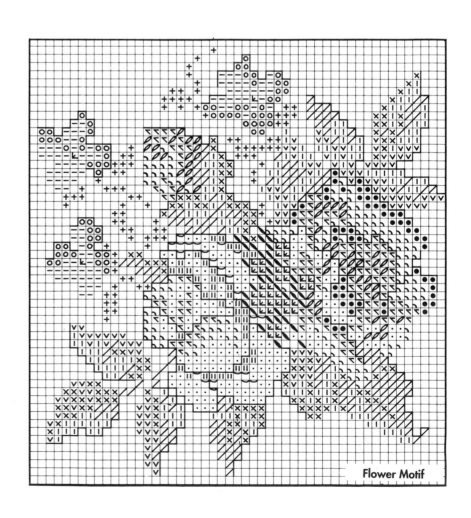

Flower Motif

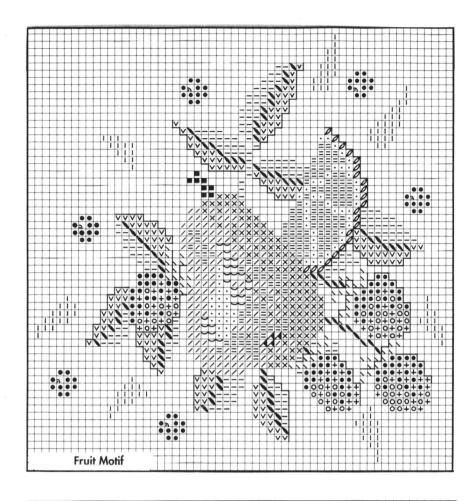

Fruit Motif

KEY TO CHART FOR
FRUIT MOTIF

KEY TO CHART FOR
FRUIT MOTIF

		Anchor	DMC
⑤	= white	1	white
⊙	= pink	26	894
⊞	= bright pink	28	8926
⊠	= red	46	666
⊡	= dark red	47	817
⊟	= light green	204	954
⊻	= green	226	703
◿	= dark green	230	911
⊔	= yellow green	254	472
⊡	= pale yellow	292	745
⊡	= light yellow	293	727
⊘	= yellow	297	726
⊟	= light orange	314	741
⊠	= orange	333	946
⊡	= brown	365	976
◨	= black	403	310
⊡	= turquoise	433	996

Stem stitch: on the leaves: dark
green 211 or 561, outline everything
else dark red.

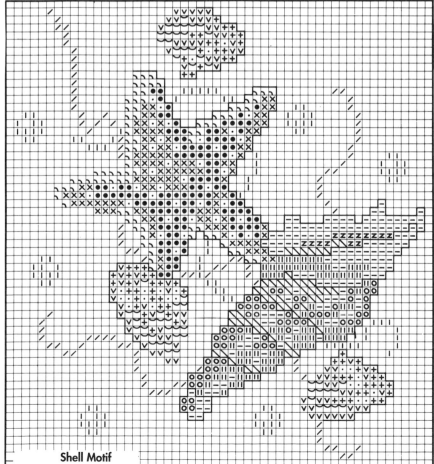

Shell Motif

KEY TO CHART FOR
SHELL MOTIF

		Anchor	DMC
⊡	= white	1	white
⊠	= pale pink	49	963
⊻	= pink	52	956
⊞	= strawberry	54	892
◿	= purple	109	210
⊡	= blue	161	334
⊞	= yellow	305	744
⊙	= salmon	313	402
◨	= dark salmon	324	721
⊠	= melon	328	3341
⊡	= rust	338	921
⊟	= soft yellow	386	746
⊡	= gray	848	928
⑤	= pale peach	881	945

Stem stitch: On the pink shell and
starfish, outline in red 46 or 666,
outline everything else in rust

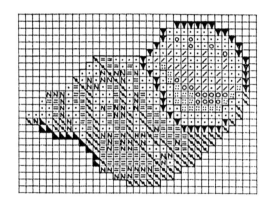

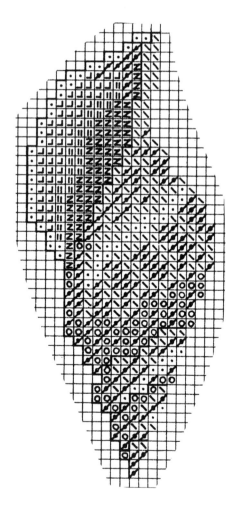

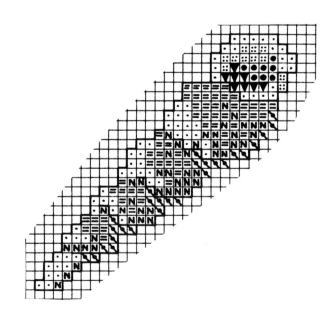

TABLECLOTH WITH SEASHELLS

PAGE 111

FINISHED MEASUREMENTS

52" x 67-1/2"

MATERIALS

2 yds of pink even-weave cloth about 59" wide with 22 threads per inch, DMC floss in indicated colors for shells. For confetti: blue #334, yellow #744, pink #604, green #954, brown #758.

INSTRUCTIONS

Embroider the shells in cross stitch by following charts. Use chart for shells on photo album for center shell and the small charts for the small shell and starfish, each stitch worked with 3 strands over 2 double threads. Place the shell motifs where you desire on the tablecloth, one in each corner. Between the shells, make small dots in satin stitch using 2 strands of floss, placed where you desire.

Cut the selvedge edge off the cloth. Embroider small cross stitches in light red #891, 4-1/2" from all edges. Leave 2 double strands between each stitch. Make a hem 1-1/2" wide with mitered corners. Hemstitch in place. ■

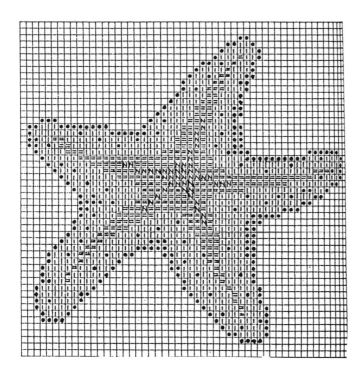

KEY TO CHART FOR
SHELL TABLECLOTH

		DMC
⊡	= white	white
☒	= light red	891
⊙	= beige	437
◩	= light yellow	745
⊟	= dark red	352
⊔	= pink	353
☒	= dark rose red	3328

PLACE MAT WITH PANSIES

PAGE 112

FINISHED MEASUREMENTS

14-1/4" x 16-1/2"

MATERIALS

Ecru linen 16" x 18-1/4" with 20 threads to the inch, Anchor embroidery floss in indicated colors plus red #011 and pink #025.

INSTRUCTIONS

Cut the linen to desired size allowing a 1/4" hem with the same size inner hem. If desired, make an openwork hem with mitered corners, gathering 2 threads in each stitch. Embroider the motif in cross stitch in the lower left and upper right corners beginning 12 threads above the open hem. Embroider the lines in satin stitch using 4 strands of floss over 2 threads. For the next border, begin 12 threads above outside border, then work the last border 12 threads above. Extend border to meet at corners. Work in red, then pink, then red floss (see photo). Embroider the narrow horizontal side in vertical satin stitch. Work the cross stitches using 4 strands of floss over 2 threads. For the stem stitches use 3 strands of floss. ■

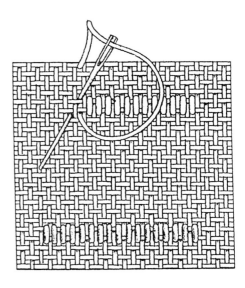

Satin Stitch Border

		Anchor
⊡	= yellow	295
◨	= light yellow	292
⊞	= bright yellow	297
⊔	= light green	266
☑	= green	258
⊠	= dark green	228
☑	= light lilac	95
⊡	= lilac	96
⊡	= dark lilac	92
⊠	= light lavender	342
⊟	= lavender	108
⊠	= dark lavender	109
☑	= purple	110
⊠	= plum	102
■	= black	403
⊡	= gray	398
⊡	= white	402

Stem stitch: on the white pansy,
embroider in gray 400, outline in
violet 100

BREAD BASKET NAPKINS

PAGE 66

FINISHED MEASUREMENTS

17-3/4" x 17-3/4"

MATERIALS

1/2 yd white Aida cloth 55" wide,
striped fabric 10" x 18", DMC embroidery floss in indicated colors and dark
green 923, white sewing thread

INSTRUCTIONS

Cut the Aida cloth to a square about
17" x 17" being sure to keep whole
blocks of threads at edges. Cut 2 strips
of striped material 17" long and 2"
wide and 2 strips 18-1/4" x 2". With
1/4" seam allowance, sew the 2 short
strips right sides together to opposite
sides of white square so that ends of
the square and the strips are even. Sew
the 2 long strips to opposite sides with
even overlapping ends. Fold short
strips to wrong side, make 1/4" hem
and sew in place. Fold long strips to
wrong side and sew in place, overlapping ends of short strips.

Embroider the motif in cross stitch by
placing the chart in the center of one
of the corners with a leaf pointing to a
corner. Use 2 strands of floss for each
cross stitch, covering 2 double threads
of cloth. Stem stitch the flowers using
2 strands of dark plum and outline in
stem stitch using 1 strand of dark
green. ■

KEY TO CHART

		DMC
⊡	= lilac	209
⊟	= light periwinkle	794
⊡	= light blue	775
☑	= periwinkle	793
⊙	= dark periwinkle	792
☑	= light green	954
⊠	= green	912
◨	= yellow green	772
⊞	= moss green	3347
◨	= yellow	445

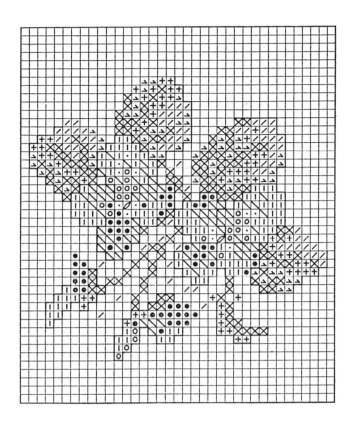

Bread basket napkin photograph on page 66.

METRIC CONVERSION CHART

Inches		Centimeters	Inches		Centimeters	Inches		Centimeters
1/4"	=	.5 cm	15"	=	38 cm	35"	=	89 cm
1/3"	=	1 cm	16"	=	41 cm	37"	=	94 cm
1/2"	=	1.5 cm	17"	=	43 cm	38"	=	97 cm
3/4"	=	2 cm	18"	=	46 cm	39"	=	99 cm
1"	=	2.5 cm	19"	=	48.5 cm	40"	=	102 cm
2"	=	5 cm	20"	=	51 cm	41"	=	104 cm
3"	=	7.5 cm	21"	=	53.5 cm	42"	=	107 cm
4"	=	10 cm	22"	=	56 cm	43"	=	109 cm
5"	=	13 cm	23"	=	58.5 cm	44"	=	112 cm
6"	=	15 cm	24"	=	61 cm	46"	=	117 cm
7"	=	18 cm	25"	=	63.5 cm	48"	=	122 cm
8"	=	20.5 cm	26"	=	66 cm	50"	=	127 cm
9"	=	23 cm	27"	=	69 cm	52"	=	132 cm
10"	=	25.5 cm	28"	=	71 cm	54"	=	137 cm
11"	=	28 cm	29"	=	74 cm	55"	=	140 cm
12"	=	30.5 cm	30"	=	76 cm	57"	=	145 cm
13"	=	33 cm	31"	=	79 cm	59"	=	150 cm
14"	=	35.5 cm	33"	=	84 cm			

INDEX